# TAMBURLAINE'S MALADY

## AND OTHER ESSAYS ON ASTROLOGY
## IN ELIZABETHAN DRAMA

# TAMBURLAINE'S
# MALADY

## AND OTHER ESSAYS ON
## ASTROLOGY
## IN ELIZABETHAN DRAMA

*by* JOHNSTONE PARR

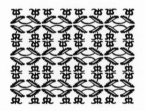

UNIVERSITY, ALABAMA

*UNIVERSITY OF ALABAMA PRESS*

*MCMLIII*

*For Mary*

# Preface

OTHERS than I have studied the subject of Elizabethan astrology. E. B. Knobel's "Astrology and Astronomy" in *Shakespeare's England* is a good general discussion of various aspects and techniques of astrology in Elizabethan times. The last two volumes of Lynn Thorndike's six-volume *History of Magic and Experimental Science* contain a vast amount of astrological data of the sixteenth and seventeenth centuries, valuable for the scholar of literature as well as for the historian. Don Cameron Allen's *The Star-Crossed Renaissance* discusses attitudes towards astrology in the sixteenth century, particularly in England. Eustace F. Bosanquet has made an outstanding bibliographical study of Elizabethan almanacks and prognostications, and Carroll Camden has published significant articles on these as well as on astrology in the Elizabethan practice of medicine. A chapter in Louis B. Wright's *Middle-Class Culture in Elizabethan England* presents the Elizabethan commoner's reaction to ephemeral books on astrology. These and a few other studies show that the pseudo-sciences of alchemy, chiromancy, physiognomy, metoposcopy, and astrology—however much they may now be considered aberrations of the human mind—were arts and sciences of considerable vogue in the Renaissance.

Since astrology in particular was reputedly entwined in the lives of men in the sixteenth century, many of the various branches of this science were frequently employed by the Elizabethan artist in the creation of his works. Rarely, however, has anyone explained the literary allusions to astrology in the Elizabethan drama in the light of astrological textbooks which appeared during the Renaissance and in the Elizabethan world. The purpose behind these essays, therefore, has been to investigate Renaissance astrological principles and techniques, apply them to significant astrological allusions of the Elizabethan and Jacobean dramatists, and thus more adequately explain and interpret such allusions in the drama of the period. My design has been to investigate how, to what extent, and with what literary or dramatic significance the playwrights have drawn upon the astrological doctrines of their time.

I have not attempted, except quite incidentally, to determine precisely what source or sources the Elizabethan playwright drew upon for his knowledge of astrology because I do not believe that such a discovery is generally probable. One must consider that the system of astrology goes back to—even beyond—the beginning of the Christian era, and that its precepts have been handed down by many men at different times and in various countries. Claudius Ptolemy's classical *Quadripartitum* or *Tetrabiblos* and the astrological works of the Arabian scientists in mediaeval Spain were published in numerous places throughout the Renaissance, and sixteenth-century astrologers who wrote of the science harked back to these astrological "masters" and copied their maxims. Some astrologers, indeed, wrote more elaborate treatises than others; some distinguished between "natural" and "artificial" astrology; some concerned themselves only with genethliac astrology, or "elections" or "interrogations" or "revolutions"; but all were practically at one on the essentials of the science. The principles of astrology are thus not to be found exclusively in the works of any single writer. I suspect, therefore, that the exact source of an Elizabethan dramatist's astrological references is almost impossible to determine with any degree of certainty.

Though I may occasionally seem to do so, I have not attempted to determine the playwright's astrological beliefs or attitudes. The Elizabethan Age harbored varied opinions regarding astrology. Pious folk held the stars to be merely the instruments of divine providence. Speculative philosophers ascribed astral influence to various occult forces at work in the macrocosm and microcosm. Some Elizabethans accepted astral influences but rejected the casting of horoscopes—perhaps because frequent inaccuracies of the astrologers made them sceptical, perhaps because their religious scruples persuaded them that it was evil to pry into God's providence. Some were sure that all astrologers dabbled with "black magic," carried on a nefarious business in dark alleys and in league with the devil. But Elizabethans in general believed almost implicitly in the *power* of the stars, even when they distrusted astrologers. As long as astrology's principles were kept within Christian limits—allowing God to be the moving power behind the stars—there were few indeed who rejected astrology outright and unconditionally.

The Elizabethan dramatists were not astrologers or scientists. They were primarily playwrights. But they were also Elizabethans, and the diverse parts of the little worlds they created in their dramas were based most frequently on materials found in the contemporary milieu. Their fictitious characters who strutted the boards and reacted to specific environments and stimulations were in large measure of the Elizabethan world—a microcosm with which the playwright, through observation and experience, had become familiar. Even in far-away or romantic settings these fictitious men and women were presented as if they were men and women in real life. The playwright observed his creation objectively, supplied characters and situations which the spectators wanted to see and hear and were able to understand. If he were a good dramatist, he permitted his characters to express whatever opinions would seem to be dramatically suitable. For this reason it is a somewhat futile procedure to reconstruct from a dramatist's plays his "personal attitude" toward his materials. Only an unwary critic would take either Edmund's strictures upon astrology in *King Lear* or Helena's assurance of astral virtues in *All's Well* to reflect Shakespeare's personal attitude.

Any dramatist is usually in eager search of the springs of human action and character, and particularly of the powers of the universe to which might be attributed human misfortunes. Whatever kind of philosopher or prober into human nature the Elizabethan dramatist might have been, he was most likely convinced that man's material life is usually not of his own choosing. And finally when a few of the dramatists focused upon human character as a progressive shaper of destiny—as did Shakespeare in his great tragedies of Hamlet, Othello, King Lear, Macbeth, and Antony—even then they did not neglect to dwell often upon other forces which shaped one's ends. The "tragedians of the city" of London had not forgotten mediaeval concepts of the goddess Fortuna, Senecan fatalism, or the stars.

Although the plays of the period are replete with astrological allusions, yet *comparatively* few of these innumerable references give specific evidence that the dramatist possessed more than a commonplace knowledge of the science. None of the dramatists appear to have been specialists in astrology as were the Harveys. Yet all of them continually refer to the power of the stars; and there is no other single topic referred to in Elizabethan drama more often—unless it be mythology. If the essays in this book do not specifically make this clear, it is because reams of sheer data from several hundred Elizabethan plays have been omitted. The plays of Lodge, Peele, Nashe, Kyd, and all the lesser playwrights abound with simple or commonplace astrological allusions. In them misfortunes are seriously but vaguely attributed to the "heavens" and the "cursed stars." Unspecified planets merely "reign" to direct one's life one way or another. The stars are stated to be "contrary" or "agreeable" or "retrograde" in the natal hour; they "conspire"; they "smile with fair aspect" and "frown with dire aspect"; they are "fatal" and "doom" one to misfortune or misery; they are "happy" and determine harmonious "effects." The "heavens" are in a hurly-burly and presage this or that; comets blaze and forewarn; the Dog Star is malignant; and so on and on. It is not expedient here to gloss or even list all references of this sort. On the other hand, in many instances we can construct a full explanation of what was in the mind of the playwright and the audience when an astrological allusion sufficed to delineate a large and complex system of procedures and activities. These are the instances which have formed the topics of these chapters.

My researches have provided me with many entertaining experiences. I have discovered that Christopher Marlowe's Tamburlaine was posssessed of a destiny already conceived for him by the planets of his horoscope, that the medical diagnosis of his illness given just before his death is replete with astrological significance, and that an explanation of his physician's diagnosis enhances considerably our knowledge of the play. I have pointed out that Mycetes' horoscope in *Tamburlaine* is especially fitting astrologically and dramatically, and I have explained the astrological "characters" which Doctor Faustus threw into his magic circle to conjure up Mephistophilis. I have noticed that John Lyly motivated properly an entire play by means of astral influences, and that Robert Greene's King James IV possessed a significant horoscope which critics of the play have overlooked. I have observed that Shakespeare grasped a large amount of quite commonplace astrological material and moulded out of an apparently superficial knowledge of the science some unusually well-integrated and exceptionally artistic lines; that he seemed well informed concerning eclipse prognostications and the astrological literature regarding them; and that his horoscope for Edmund in *King Lear* explains much of this ill-gotten son's character and activities. I have showed how George Chapman dramatically blamed the Duke of Byron's unfortunate end at least partly on a malignant configuration in the Duke's natal horoscope, and how John Webster employed horoscope-casting to add verisimilitude to his play about the Malfi family. I have discussed instances wherein Ben Jonson used astrology and similar non-alchemical sciences in his play dealing principally with alchemy. I have been amazed in discovering the large number of astrological writers and astrological publications current in Europe in the sixteenth century, and have presented a chapter on these publications and briefly accounted for the materials in them—particularly those which made their way into England. In addition I provide a fairly complete bibliography of such works for the years 1473–1625 which I have spent much time compiling over a period of ten years. But the greatest entertainment of all has been the experience of discovering that much in Elizabethan and Jacobean drama can be better understood by observing the principles lying behind many astrological allusions in these plays. I hope I have made it possible for others to read these plays with a greater degree of understanding and appreciation.

Six of the thirteen essays (about one-third of the book) have been published previously in the *Publications of the Modern Language Association*, the *Studies in Philology*, the *Philological Quarterly*, and the *Shakespeare Association Bulletin*, which I am grateful to be able to reprint. I was first introduced to astrology in English literature by Professor Hudson Strode, of the University of Alabama. Subsequently I studied under Professor Walter Clyde Curry, at Vanderbilt University, where a considerable portion of this work was submitted as a doctoral dissertation in 1941. To both of these men—as teachers, scholars, models, and advisers—my indebtedness is very large. The University of Alabama Research Committee awarded me several grants-in-aid for the purchase of microfilm and photostats, for which I am grateful. I am greatly obligated also to Professor Lynn Thorndike, of Columbia University, whom I have never met, and who knows me not, but whose work has immeasurably influenced mine.

J. P.

*Tuscaloosa, Alabama*
*March, 1953*

# CONTENTS

## *JOHN WEBSTER*

## *BEN JONSON*

## *BIBLIOGRAPHY*

# Tamburlaine's Malady

## And Other Essays on Astrology
## in Elizabethan Drama

## CHAPTER ONE

# TAMBURLAINE'S MALADY

THE CONSIDERABLE AMOUNT of commentary published on Marlowe's
Tamburlaine in recent years makes highly significant the fact that
Tamburlaine's catastrophe remains one of the unsatisfactorily explained enigmas of the play. The unwary reader doubtless assumes
that at the end of *Tamburlaine II* the Scythian conqueror simply—
though somewhat vitriolically—dies, and that Marlowe should be
called to account for marring his play with a badly-motivated catastrophe. The careful reader of Marlowe's text doubtless perceives (or at
least suspects) that Tamburlaine's "distemper" at the end of the play
is linked definitely with Renaissance medical, physiological, psychological, and astrological concepts. Yet no satisfactory analysis of how
these concepts are involved in Tamburlaine's death has been made.[1]
Carroll Camden hazards the suggestion that Tamburlaine's death is
immediately resultant upon his choleric humour.[2] Miss Una Ellis-
Fermor, the most recent editor of *Tamburlaine,* attempts to supply
proper annotation regarding the physician's diagnosis of Tamburlaine's
"distemper," but her footnotes are inadequate as well as inaccurate.[3]
Don Cameron Allen, believing that "Marlowe conceived of his hero
as a typical representative of the *fortunati*,"[4] a Renaissance type of
fortunate man upon whom Fortune never failed to smile, contends
mistakenly that Tamburlaine comes to no catastrophe at all but tri-

[1] Carroll Camden's articles, "Marlowe and Elizabethan Psychology," *PQ*, VIII
(1929), 69–78, and "Tamburlaine: The Choleric Man," *MLN*, XLIV (1929), 430–
435, do not (I hope to show) satisfactorily explain Tamburlaine's malady.
[2] *PQ*, p. 77.
[3] *Tamburlaine the Great* (Methuen & Co., London, 1930), pp. 273–274.
[4] "Renaissance Remedies for Fortune: Marlowe and the *Fortunati*," *SP*,
XXXVIII (1941), 195.

umphantly "dies of old age."[5] Roy W. Battenhouse has considered
Tamburlaine an instrument by means of which God, in His provi-
dential justice, scourges the world, and then, when the mundane
chastisement is completed, strikes down His tyrannical instrument.[6]
Although in this article Professor Battenhouse does not explain, or
even consider, the express bodily workings of Tamburlaine's malady,
in his subsequent book[7] he assumes (following Camden) that Tamburlaine is—among other things—a typical choleric man, and affirms
that the physician's diagnosis indicates that Tamburlaine dies in a mad
frenzy brought on by that disastrous affliction of the "humours" which
Elizabethans termed *choler adust*.

The interpretation by Professor Allen ignores the physician's diagnosis, and the interpretations of Professors Camden, Battenhouse, and
Ellis-Fermor are based upon a complete misunderstanding of some
pertinent words in Marlowe's text. For the physician's diagnosis *says
nothing whatever about the choleric humour*. I do not wish to detract
from the general idea in these interesting interpretations. It could be
that in bodying forth his character of the Scythian tyrant Marlowe had
all of them in mind. But I do wish to point out another possible and
plausible interpretation, and to correct these commentators on the
physician's diagnosis of Tamburlaine's malady. My purpose in this
chapter is (1) to suggest that Tamburlaine's inordinate and innate
passions (and incidentally his stars) precipitate his death, and (2) to
explain fully the medical, psycho-physiological, and astrological concepts mentioned by Tamburlaine's physician and, therefore, specifically involved in the conqueror's decease.

I

Marlowe presents Tamburlaine as a gigantic and energetic man lust-
ing for military dominion, believing in his own destiny, and withal
being particularly cruel, proud, and wrathful; and he definitely links
Tamburlaine's reiterated invincibility with the impelling power of the

[5] *Ibid.*, p. 197.
[6] "Tamburlaine, the 'Scourge of God,'" *PMLA*, LVI (1941), 337–348.
[7] *Marlowe's Tamburlaine, A Study in Renaissance Moral Philosophy* (Nash-
ville: Vanderbilt University Press, 1941), pp. 174 ff., 217 ff.

stars.[8] All of these physical qualities, mental characteristics, and cosmological concepts Marlowe found in his sources.[9] But he did not get specifically from his source material the cause and the manner of Tamburlaine's death; for the acknowledged sources of the play state that in the full vigor of his life the great Scythian died a peaceful and natural death in Samarcand.[10] Undoubtedly not wanting to foist on his audience a unique catastrophe incompatible with the histories, Marlowe had to fabricate adroitly a reasonable manner in which to dispatch his hero and at the same time stay within the bounds of historical expediency. Having allowed his hero in *Tamburlaine I* to become gloriously invincible and heavenly-guarded in military affairs, Marlowe doubtless decided that the only appropriate conqueror of Tamburlaine should be Tamburlaine himself. Accordingly he allowed his wrathful Scythian to die from a malignant "distemper" which might be brought on as a result of his fiery temperament.[11]

From various mediaeval and Renaissance treatises we may gather that violent passions can cause malignant distempers of the body. Virtually all the classical and mediaeval physicians stated that abnormal emotion (anger, for example) can produce fevers.[12] The *De occulta*

[8] Throughout both parts of *Tamburlaine* not only Tamburlaine but also his friends and some of his enemies exclaim knowingly that the great Scythian is fated by the stars to succeed in his conquests. (See *Tamburlaine I*, i.ii.91–92; ii.i.33–34; iii.iii.41–43; iv.ii.33–34; v.ii.167–171, 296–297; *Tamburlaine II*, iii.v. 79–89. All references and citations herein are from Miss Ellis-Fermor's edition, *op. cit.*). Professor Allen (*op. cit.*), as well as almost all other commentators, has noticed particularly this aspect of Tamburlaine's career.

[9] See the discussion of Marlowe's sources in Ellis-Fermor, *op. cit.*, pp. 17 ff. Cf. also H. C. Hart, "Tamburlaine and Primaudaye," *Notes and Queries*, 10th Series, v (January-June 1906), 484–487, 504–506; Ethel Seaton, "Fresh Sources for Marlowe," *RES*, v 1929), 385–401; Leslie Spence, "The Influence of Marlowe's Sources on Tamburlaine I," *MP*, xxiv (1926), 181–199, and "Tamburlaine and Marlowe," *PMLA*, xlii (1927), 604–622.

[10] Miss Seaton (*op. cit.*, p. 398) points out that in Andre Thevet's *Cosmographie Universelle* (1575) three portents—a man with a spear, a comet, and the ghost of Bajazet—manifest themselves at Tamburlaine's death. The last portent in Thevet's account supposedly terrified Tamburlaine to death.

[11] Leslie Spence (*PMLA*, xlii, 621) suggests this premise but not the conclusion.

[12] Cf. Francis Adams, *The Seven Books of Paulus Aegineta*, trans. from the Greek, 3 vols. (London, 1844), i, 229 ff. Among the causes of ephemeral fevers Galen listed "sorrow, fear, anxiety, and depressing passions," and Paulus Aegineta included "cares, grief, watchfulness, and anger." *Ibid.*, pp. 229–231. One of the four classes of ephemeral fevers designated by the Arabian Haly Abbas included

*philosophia* of Henry Cornelius Agrippa, who drew immeasurably upon the physicians and other wise men of the early Renaissance, contains several chapters under such captions as "The Passions of the Mind and the Soul Can Change the Proper Body." Agrippa writes, for instance:

The passions of the soul are the chiefest cause of the temperament of its proper body. So the soul, being strongly elevated, and inflamed with a strong imagination, sends forth health or sickness in its proper body. . . . To these things Avicen, Aristotle, Algazel, and Gallen assent.[13]

The passions . . . change the proper body with a sensible transmutation, by changing the accidents of the body, and by moving the spirits upward or downward, inward or outward, and by producing divers qualities in the members. So in joy, the spirits are driven outward; in fear, drawn back; in bashfulness, are moved to the brain. . . . After the same manner in anger or fear, but suddenly. Again, anger, or desire for revenge, produceth heat, redness, a bitter taste and a looseness. Fear induceth cold, trembling of the heart, speechlessness and paleness. Sadness causeth sweat and a bluish whiteness. Pity, which is a kind of sadness, doth often ill affect the body. . . . Anxiety induceth dryness and blackness. And how great heats love stirs up in the liver and pulse, physicians know. . . . It is also manifest that such like passions, when they are most vehement, may cause death. And this is manifest to all men that with too much joy, sadness, love, or hatred, men many times die. And so we read that Sophocles, and Dionysius, the Silician tyrant, did both suddenly die at the news of a tragical victory. So a certain woman, also, seeing her son returning from the Canensian battle, died suddenly. . . . Sometimes, also, by reason of these like passions, long diseases follow. . . . And how much vehement anger, joined with great audacity, can do, Alexander the Great shows, who, being circumvented with a battle in India, was seen to send forth from himself lightning and fire; the father

---

those caused by "violent passions, such as anger, fear, and the like." *Ibid.*, pp. 233–234. Averrhoes, Avenzoar, Avicenna, Rhases, and Rogerius make similar statements, servilely adopting the views of the more ancient physicians (*Ibid.*, pp. 229–235); and in turn the majority of the Renaissance physicians inherited and adopted the same precepts. Indeed, so little had the Vesalian theories superseded the traditional Galenic physiology that we find Jeremy Collier in the seventeenth century often observing that emotional states "boil up the Blood to a Fever." Cf. Kathleen Ressler, *Jeremy Collier's Essays,* in *Seventeenth Century Studies,* Second Series (Princeton University Press, 1937), p. 219.

[13] Henry Cornelius Agrippa von Nettesheim, *Three Books of Occult Philosophy or Magic,* trans. by J. F. (London, 1651), Bk. 1, Ch. lxv. I cite from Willis F. Whitehead's reproduction of J. F.'s translation (New York, 1897), pp. 200–201.

of Theodoricus is said to have sent forth out of his body sparks of fire, so that sparkling flames did leap out with a noise.[14]

Numerous other sixteenth-century treatises give evidence that Elizabethans were well aware that passions produce physiological changes in the body and its working organisms. Pierre Charron writes:

*Anger* makes the Blood boil in our hearts, and raises wild and furious Vapours in our Mind. . . . The signs and Symptoms of this Passion make a mighty difference in the Person, alter the whole Temper and Frame both of Body and Mind, transform and turn him into quite another man. Some of these changes and Symptoms are outward and apparent: Redness and Distortions of the Face, Fieryness of the Eyes, a wild and enraged look, . . . quickness and unevenness of the Pulse, Swelling and bursting of the Veins, . . . and in short, the whole Body is set on Fire, and in a perfect Fever. Some have been transported to such a degree . . . that their very Veins have broke, their Urine stopt, and they have dropt down dead, being stifled and strangled with excess of Passion.[15]

Thomas Wright remarks at the beginning of his treatise entitled *The Passions of the minde in generall:*

. . . for there is no Passion very vehement, but that it alters extreamely some of the four humours of the bodie; and all Physitians commonly agree, that among diverse other extrinsecall causes of diseases one, and not the least, is, the excesse of some inordinate Passion.[16]

Sir Thomas Elyot explains the results of anger and ire as follows:

Of this affection cometh sometyme fevers, sometyme, apoplexies, or privation of sences, tremblynge, palseys, madnesse, fransies, deformytie of vysage: and that wars [worse] is, outragious swearynge, blaspheyme, desyre of vengeance. . . .[17]

La Primaudaye tells us that fear may wreak havoc upon the body:

Yea a great and sudden feare, because all the blood retiring to the heart chaoketh it, and utterly extinguisheth natural heate and the spirits, so that death must needes ensue thereof.[18]

---

[14] *Ibid.*, Bk. I, Ch. lxiii, pp. 195–197.

[15] *Of Wisdom, Three Books, Written Originally in French by the Sieur de Charron, Made English by George Stanhope, D.D.* (London, 1697), pp. 205–208. The original, *De la Sagesse,* was published at Bordeaux in 1601; there existed a contemporary English translation by Samson Lennard. For further references in Charron, see pp. 213, 217–18, 230–231, 238.

[16] (London, 1604), p. 4. See also the 1601 edition, p. 86.

[17] *The Castel of Health* (London, 1547), 64 v.

[18] *The French Academie* (London, 1594), p. 471.

It was common knowledge, therefore, among sixteenth-century intel-
lectuals that passions could initiate all sorts of bodily distempers and
bring one ultimately to ruin.[19] Keeping in mind this tenet of Elizabethan psycho-physiology, let us examine Tamburlaine's catastrophe.

Toward the end of *Tamburlaine II* the Scythian conqueror's enemies
deliver themselves of several uncomplimentary epithets regarding
Tamburlaine's violent and unmerciful onslaughts. The King of Jeru-
salem, affording us a premonition that Tamburlaine shall be punished
by the heavens, cries out:

> Thy victories are grown so violent,
> That shortly heaven, filled with meteors
> Of blood and fire thy tyrannies have made,
> Will pour down blood and fire on thy head,
> Whose scalding drops will pierce thy seething brains,
> And with our bloods revenge our bloods on thee.[20]

And the King of Soria gives us a hint as to what shall happen to
Tamburlaine when the former exclaims:

> May never spirit, vein or artier feed
> The cursed substance of that cruel heart;
> But, wanting moisture and remorseful blood,
> Dry up with anger and consume with heat![21]

These men have ample reason to regard Tamburlaine thus, for his
inordinate lust for conquest and his fiery temperament have indeed led
the seemingly invincible Scythian to ravage, pillage, and devastate. Particularly after the death of Zenocrate (II, iv), his raging anger attains a
noticeable crescendo. He consumes with fire the town Zenocrate died
in simply because he believes that the place itself bereft him of his
love.[22] He burns continually thereafter with an increasing ardor for
conquest; he devises harrowing punishments for his enemies; his
"wrathful looks"[23] and his eyes "composed of fury and of fire"[24]
presage death to those who stand in his way. Eventually his violent

---

[19] For further information on the actions of the passions, see particularly Ruth
Leila Anderson's *Elizabethan Psychology and Shakespeare's Plays,* University of
Iowa Studies (Iowa City, 1927), and Lily B. Campbell's *Shakespeare's Tragic
Heroes, Slaves of Passion* (Cambridge University Press, 1930), and the array of
bibliographical items which they cite.

[20] IV.i.140–145.     [21] IV.i.178–181.     [22] II.iv.137–138; III.ii.1–14.     [23] III.v.119.
[24] IV.i.176.

wrath and anger—specifically mentioned innumerable times—become so unbridled that he murders his own son merely because the boy fails to participate in battle.[25] After hanging the Babylonian governor and unmercifully riddling this official's body with bullets, Tamburlaine orders his soldiers to sack the city and drown in Asphaltis Lake "every man, woman, and child"[26] who lives in Babylon. This his soldiers do until the fishes are well-nigh choked.[27]

Suddenly, amid these frenzied outbursts in which Tamburlaine considers himself the "wrathful messenger of mighty Jove,"[28] the raging conquerer is "distempered"—from what, he knows not.[29] But shortly thereafter we find in the remarks of Theridamas a hint as to the nature of Tamburlaine's illness:

> Weep, heavens, and vanish into liquid tears!
> Fall, stars that govern his nativity,
> And summon all the shining lamps of heaven
> To cast their bootless fires to the earth,
> And shed their feeble influence in the air;
> Muffle your beauties with eternal clouds,
> For hell and darkness pitch their pitchy tents,
> And Death, with armies of Cimmerian spirits,
> Gives battle 'gainst the heart of Tamburlaine.
> Now, in defiance of that wonted love
> Your sacred virtues pour'd upon his throne,
> And made his state an honour to the heavens,
> These cowards invisibly assail his soul,
> And threaten conquest on our sovereign;
> But if he die, your glories are disgrac'd,
> Earth droops and says that hell in heaven is placed.[30]

Theridamas, we notice, specifically asks the fortunate stars of Tamburlaine's natal horoscope to assert their power and overcome the "armies of Cimmerian spirits" as they "battle" against the conqueror's heart. But in spite of this and other pleas by Tamburlaine's henchmen,[31] the torments of the conqueror increase. He knows that he shall die. Perhaps he knows that the "Cimmerian spirits," the "invisible cowards,"

---

[25] iv.i.120.    [26] v.i.169.    [27] v.i.202–208.    [28] v.i.92.    [29] v.i.217–219.
[30] v.iii.1–16.

[31] Techelles and Usumcasane also pray that the heavenly powers shall continue to pour out their good influences on the life and health of Tamburlaine. See v.iii.17–41.

are causing all the trouble. But apparently he does not know that his
passion is the root of the evil; or if he does, he cannot check himself,
for he resumes unhesitatingly his attempts to be "the terror of the
world." He continues to rave of war and revenge:

> Come, let us march against the powers of Heaven,
> And set black streamers in the firmament,
> To signify the slaughter of the gods.
> Ah, friends, what shall I do? I cannot stand.
> Come, carry me to war against the gods,
> That thus envy the health of Tamburlaine.[32]

Theridamas, perhaps understanding that Tamburlaine's passion is
probably the source of his illness, admonishes:

> Ah, good my lord, leave these impatient words,
> Which add much danger to your malady![33]

But Tamburlaine, as fiery as ever, replies that "in revenge of this [his
pain]" [34] he will forestall "the ugly monster death" [35] by getting immediately to the battlefield, where

> I and mine army come to load thy bark
> With souls of thousand mangled carcasses.
>
> . . . . . . . . . . . . . .
> . . . . . . Techelles, let us march,
> And weary Death with bearing souls to hell.[36]

Tamburlaine's physician then attempts to calm him. He administers
medicine and pronounces his diagnosis that Tamburlaine's state of
health is perilous indeed:

> Pleaseth your majesty to drink this potion,
> Which will abate the fury of your fit,
> And cause some milder spirits govern you.
>
> . . . . . . . . . . . . . .
> I view'd your urine, and the hypostasis,
> Thick and obscure, doth make your danger great;
> Your veins are full of accidental heat,
> Whereby the moisture of your blood is dried:
> The humidum and calor, which some hold
> Is not a parcel of the elements,
> But of a substance more divine and pure,
> Is almost clean extinguished and spent;

[32] v.iii.48–53.      [33] v.iii.54–55.      [34] v.iii.57.      [35] v.iii.67.      [36] v.iii.74–77.

> Which, being the cause of life, imports your death.
> Besides, my lord, this day is critical,
> Dangerous to those whose crisis is as yours:
> Your artiers, which alongst the veins convey
> The lively spirits which the heart engenders,
> Are parched and void of spirit, that the soul,
> Wanting those organons by which it moves,
> Cannot endure, by argument of art.
> Yet, if your majesty may escape this day,
> No doubt but you shall soon recover all.[37]

But Tamburlaine does not recover. A messenger enters to announce that Callapine's freshly-gathered army is ready to set upon them. Rising in agony from his couch, Tamburlaine rejoices that he may again vent his anger and (so he thinks) stave off death:

> See, my physicians, now, how Jove hath sent
> A present medicine to recure my pain.
> My looks shall make them fly; . . . .
> . . . . . . . . . Draw, you slaves!
> In spite of death, I will go show my face.[38]

In such a rage he does indeed put his opponents to flight, but he then perceives that all his martial strength is spent:

> In vain I strive and rail against those powers
> That mean t'invest me in a higher throne,[39]

But he cannot check his passion for conquest even after this admission. He calls for a map, that he may see how much of the world is left for him to overwhelm. And with his last breath he urges his son to be one like him, a wrathful, uncompromising conqueror of the world, a "scourge of God." Thus the vitriolic conqueror's violent outbursts have precipitated and perpetuated such a malignant malady that even his hitherto auspicious stars are powerless to mitigate the illness which rapidly overwhelms him.

Tamburlaine's end is, therefore, quite adequately motivated if we consider that his dominant characteristic is his inordinate passion—the passion of ambition, hatred, wrath, and revenge—from which the Elizabethan readily perceived that devastating results may be wrought upon the body. In thus allowing his gigantic and powerful character to die suddenly from some peculiar "distemper," Marlowe has not (as

[37] v.iii.78–99.     [38] v.iii.105–114.     [39] v.iii.120–121.

Horace might say) "brought on the gods." The catastrophe of Tamburlaine is not at all out of joint with his character; for his peculiar distemper has been occasioned by his innate passions, and in the light of sixteenth-century psycho-physiology it was perfectly obvious to an intelligent Elizabethan that the wrathful Scythian should have been dispatched in such a manner.

II

We have not yet properly explained the physiological nature of the malignancy which kills the Scythian tyrant—or, in short, analyzed the physician's devastating verdict to discover precisely what happens in Tamburlaine's dying body. Let us attempt to analyze adequately this medical diagnosis.

Tamburlaine's malady is undoubtedly of a febrile nature. The King of Soria remarks significantly—if his words may be taken as premonitory—that Tamburlaine's heart shall "dry up with anger and consume with heat." The physician mentions that the "heat" in Tamburlaine's veins had dried up the moisture of his blood. Tamburlaine's son Amyras, ascending his father's throne while Tamburlaine is in the very jaws of death, refers to his father's "burning agony."[40] And, as we have seen (footnote 12), classical and Elizabethan physicians were agreed that fevers could result from such violent passions as those with which Tamburlaine seems to be possessed. Undoubtedly we may conclude that Tamburlaine has contracted a fever, or at least some distemper of a febrile nature.

The physician has reported first that the "hypostasis" of Tamburlaine's water is "thick and obscure." All the classical medical authorities discuss in detail the different appearances and substances of the sick man's urinal discharges, and the indications which may be gleaned therefrom.[41] Besides the watery portion, there were three variegated substances to be distinguished in the urine: the *hypostasis* (or the sediment), the *enaeorema* (or substances which float in the watery part),

[40] v.iii.209.

[41] Cf. Francis Adams, *op. cit.,* 1, 225 ff. Adams has annexed to each section of his translation of Paulus Aegineta voluminous commentary which reports on similar medical judgments by all the authorities from Hippocrates to the late mediaeval physicians.

and the *nubeculae* (or scum which floats on the surface).[42] All of the learned doctors are agreed that the *hypostasis* is of the most importance in determining the diagnosis.[43] And Hippocrates, perhaps the supreme authority, records in his *De prognostics:*

The urine is best when the sediment is white, smooth, and consistent during the whole time, until the disease comes to a crisis, for it indicates freedom from danger, and an illness of short duration. . . . But if the urine be reddish, and the sediment consistent and smooth, the affection in this case will be protracted but still not fatal. But farinaceous sediments in the urine are bad, and still worse are the leafy; and white and thin are very bad, but the furfurcaceous are still worse than these. Clouds carried about in the urine are good when white, but bad when black. When the urine is yellow and thin, it indicates that the disease is unconcocted. . . . But the most deadly of all kinds of urine are the fetid, watery, *black* and *thick;* . . .[44]

Though the cordial administered by the physician seems in Tamburlaine's case to be of no avail, Tamburlaine's physician knows his business at least in prognosticating that an *hypostasis* "Thick and obscure, doth make your danger great," and indeed has due cause to be alarmed.

Tamburlaine's physician hopes that the medicinal potion will "cause some milder spirits" to "govern" his patient, and remarks further:

> Your artiers, which alongst the veins convey
> The lively spirits, which the heart engenders,
> Are parched and void of spirit, that the soul,
> Wanting those organons by which it moves,
> Cannot endure, by argument of art.

Innumerable Elizabethan treatises explain in detail the manner in which the *soul* and the *spirits* function in the human body.[45] The soul, they maintain, is provided with three distinct faculties: vegetative, sensible, and rational. It gives to the body its life, motion, and sense through its association with the three principal organs of the body: the liver, the heart, and the brain. The vegetative faculty, provided by the liver, promotes nutrition, growth, and reproduction; the sensible faculty, provided by the heart, promotes the body's motions and desires;

---

[42] *Ibid.,* pp. 225–226.

[43] *Ibid.,* p. 226. Paulus Aegineta records specifically: "Of these characters, the sediment is of the most importance."

[44] *The Genuine Works of Hippocrates,* trans. from the Greek by Francis Adams (New York, n.d.), I, 202–203.

[45] Cf. Anderson, *op. cit.,* chs. iii and vii; Campbell, *op. cit.,* chs. vi and viii; and the authorities which these two cite.

the rational faculty, provided by the brain, promotes the intellectual appetites and reason. But in order to make possible these operations, the body is provided with certain fumes or vapors or substances known as *spirits*. Bartholomaeus Anglicus' treatment of these is lengthy and explicit:

A spirit is called a certain substance, subtle and airy, that stirreth and exciteth the virtues of the body to their doings and works. . . . Physicians say that this spirit is gendered in this manner wise. Whiles by heat working in the blood, in the liver is caused strong boiling and seething, and thereof cometh a smoke, the which is pured, and made subtle in the veins of the liver. And turneth into a subtle spiritual substance and airly kind, and that is called the *natural* spirit. It maketh the blood subtle, and by lightness thereof it moveth the blood and sendeth it about and into all the limbs. And this same spirit turneth to heartward by certain veins. And there by moving and smiting together of the parts of the heart, the spirit is more pured, and turneth into a more subtle kind. And then it is called of physicians the *vital* spirit: because that from the heart, by the wosen and veins and small ways, it spreadeth itself into all the limbs of the body, and increases the virtues spiritual, and ruleth and keepeth the works thereof. . . . And so the vital spirit is spread into all the body and worketh in the artery veins the pulses of life. . . . The same spirit piercing and passing forth to the dens of the brain, is there more directed and made subtle, and is changed into the *animal* spirit, which is more subtle than the other. And so this animal spirit is gendered in the foremost den of the brain, and is spread into the limbs of feeling. But yet nevertheless some part thereof abideth in the aforesaid dens, that common sense, the common wit, the virtue imaginative, the intellect and understanding, and the memory may be made perfect. From the hindermost parts of the brain he (the spirit) passeth by the marrow of the ridge bone, and cometh to the sinews of moving, so that wilful moving may be engendered, in all parts of the nether body. Then one and the same spirit is named by divers names. For by working in the liver it is called the natural spirit, in the heart the vital spirit, and in the head, the animal spirit. We may not believe that this spirit is man's reasonable soul, but more smoothly, as saith Austin, the car therof and proper instrument. For by means of such a spirit the soul is joined to the body: and without the service of such a spirit, no act the soul may perfectly exercise in the body. And therefore if these spirits be impaired, or let of their working in any work, the accord of the body and soul is resolved, the reasonable spirit is let of all its works in the body. As it is seen in them that be amazed, and mad men and frantic, and in others that oft lose use of reason.[46]

[46] Robert Steele, *Mediaeval Lore from Bartholomaeus Anglicus* (London, 1924), pp. 28–31. Steele has produced selections from the Berthelet edition of Bartholo-

Before completing our discussion of the *spirits,* we must consider
also the doctrine that man's body contains *vital moisture* and *natural
heat.* Thomas Newton writes:

For seeing there bee three especiall thinges, in whose temperature and
moderation the health of man's body doth principally consist, viz. vitall
moysture, natural heate, & Spirite, which combineth all thinges, and im-
parteth his force, vertue & nature, unto them. . . . Vitall moysture is the
nourishment and matter of natural heate, whereupon it worketh, and by
the benefite therof is maintained and preserved. With this Humour or vitall
moysture, is natural heate fed and cherished, and from the same receyveth
continuall mayntenaunce, and from it participateth vital power, whereby all
Creatures do live, are nourished, encreased, preserved & procreated.[47]

Robert Burton agrees:

To the preservation of life the natural heat is more requisite. In all bodies
it must have the radical moisture to preserve it, that it be not consumed. For
as this natural heat and moisture decays, so doth our life itself.[48]

Then Burton adds to his statement a footnote: *"Vita consistit in calido
et humido."*

Now these statements concerning the vital (or radical) moisture and
natural heat throw some light upon the physician's warning to Tamburlaine:

> The humidum and calor, which some hold
> Is not a parcel of the elements,
> But of a substance more divine and pure,
> Is almost clean extinguished and spent;
> Which, being the cause of life, imports your death.

The *humidum* and *calor* which Tamburlaine's body lacked were, in
the Elizabethan physician's repertory, the radical moisture (known
also as the *humidum radical* or *humidum primigenium*) and the innate body heat (called *calidum innatum*). An early medical dictionary
gives the following definitions:

maeus' *De Proprietatibus Rerum* (London, 1535). For similar remarks on the
spirits, cf. Pierre Charron, *op. cit.,* pp. 26 ff.; Timothy Bright, *A Treatise of Melancholy* (London, 1586), pp. 54 ff.; John Jones, *Bathes of Bathes Ayde* (London,
1572); Robert Burton, *The Anatomy of Melancholy* (London, 1621), Part 1, Section 1, Memb. 11.

[47] *The Touchstone of Complexions* (London, 1565, 1576, 1581), ch. ii, p. 7;
quoted by Campbell, *op. cit.,* p. 55.

[48] *Op. cit.,* Part 1, Sect. 1, Memb. 11, Subj. 5.

CALOR, *Heat. c. Animalis, Animal heat.*[49]

ANIMAL HEAT. *Calor animalis, Calor nativus, Calidum animale, Calidum innatum* . . . the caloric constantly formed by the body of a living animal by virtue of which it preserves nearly the same temperature.[50]

HUMIDUM RADICALE, *Humidum primigenium, Radical Moisture.* This name was formerly given to the liquid which, by means of the circulation, was conceived to give flexibility and proper consistence to the different organic textures.[51]

A 1656 definition in Stanley's *Historical Philosophy* (1701; VI, 260–261) is especially pertinent: "Death . . . cometh . . . when through want of Refrigeration the Radical Humidity is consumed and dried up." [52] And Charron informs us specifically that the *humidum* and *calor* create the *spirits:*

The Spirits, . . . are a sort of generous Fumes, evaporated by the Natural Heat, and Radical Moisture; and of these there are Three degrees of Excellency, the Natural, the Vital, and the Animal.[53]

It was principally in order to refute this theory of anatomical *spirits* and the divine efficacy of the *calidum innatum* and to advance the hypothesis that blood and blood alone is contained in the arteries that William Harvey published his tract *On the Circulation of the Blood* in 1628. Some of Harvey's remarks on the *spirits* and the *calidum innatum* are applicable here and informing:

As frequent mention has been made in the preceding pages of the *calidum innatum,* or innate heat, I have determined to say a few words here . . . both on that subject and on the *humidum primigenium,* or radical moisture, to which I am all the more inclined because I observe that many pride themselves upon the use of these terms without, as I apprehend, rightly understanding their meaning. There is, in fact, no occasion for searching after spirits foreign to, or distant from, the blood; to evoke heat from an-

---

[49] Robley Dunglison, *A Dictionary of Medical Science* (Philadelphia: Lea and Blanchard, 4th ed., 1844), p. 123. Cf. also Bartholomew Parr, *The London Medical Dictionary* (Philadelphia, 1819), I, 314: "*Calidum innatum* is an expression borrowed from the Stoical philosophy to express the natural heat of animals, which, as connected with life, has also been called βιοηυχνιον, the lamp of life."

[50] Dunglison, *op. cit.,* pp. 47–48.

[51] *Ibid.,* p. 366.

[52] See under *Humidity* in *A New English Dictionary on Historical Principles* (ed. James A. H. Murray; Oxford, 1901), vol. v, Part 1, p. 499.

[53] *Op. cit.,* p. 26. Cf. Newton, *op. cit.,* ch. ii, for a full discussion of the relation of the spirits to health.

other source; to bring gods upon the scene, and to encumber philosophy with any fanciful conceits; what we are wont to derive from the stars is in truth produced at home; the blood is the only *calidum innatum,* or first engendered animal heat.[54]

They who descant on the *calidum innatum* or innate heat . . . take refuge in spirits as most subtile substances. These persons see . . . the natural operations as proceeding from the instrumentality of this common agent, viz. the *calidum innatum:* they further regard these spirits as of a sublime, lucid, ethereal, celestial, or divine nature, and the bond of the soul. . . . Whence they declare that the heat perpetually flowing into the several parts is in virtue of the influx of spirits through the channels of the arteries . . . and they . . . maintain . . . that the arteries are filled with such aereal spirits, and not with blood.[55]

But as it is thought that the spirits, and the ultimate or primigenial element, or something else, is contained in animals which acts in a greater degree than the blood above the forces of the elements, we are not sufficiently informed what is understood by the expression "acting above the forces of the elements"; neither are Aristotle's words rightly interpreted where he says (*De Gen. Anim.* lib. ii, cap. 3) "Every virtue or faculty of the soul appears to partake of another body more divine than those which are called elements. . . . For there is in every seed a certain something which causes it to be fruitful, viz. what is called heat, and that not fire or any faculty of the kind, but a spirit such as is contained in the semen; . . . and the nature inherent in that spirit is responsible in its proportions to the element of the stars." Now I maintain the same things of the innate heat and the blood. . . . They share the nature of a more divine body or substance. . . . There is a spirit, or certain force, inherent in the blood, acting superiorly to the powers of the elements; . . . and the nature, yea, the soul of this spirit and blood, is identical with the essence of the stars.[56]

It is apparent that Marlowe's expression of the *calor's* being "more divine and pure" than the "elements" was a common one derived ultimately from Aristotle; and that not only the *calor* but also the *spirits* were in nature *identical with the essence of the stars.* All Elizabethans, therefore, possessed in their bodies an ingredient which might be characterized as virtually a piece of a star.[57]

[54] "The Generation of Animals," in *The Works of William Harvey, M.D.,* trans. Robert Willis (London, 1847), pp. 501–502.
[55] "A Second Disquisition to John Riolan, Jun.," *The Works of William Harvey* (note 54), pp. 119–120; see also pp. 10–12, 114 ff.
[56] "The Generation of Animals," pp. 505–506.
[57] These concepts which Harvey decries were in Marlowe's day authoritative ones, for Harvey continues: "Scaliger, Fornilius, and others, giving less regard to

*Calor,* therefore, is not to be confused with *choler.* The latter was one of the fluids known as the four "humours," which were generated in the blood by the admixture of food and drink and the four elements.[58] *Choler* was not (as Tamburlaine's physician says *calor* is) "the cause of life" or "more divine and pure than the elements," and was not (so far as I know) ever spoken of as complementary with *humidum;* whereas all of these requirements of Tamburlaine's *calor* may be satisfied by substituting the term *calidum innatum.* In view of these facts, the preceding definitions, the remarks of Burton and Harvey, and the fact that Marlowe actually used the word *choler* elsewhere in *Tamburlaine,*[59] it seems fairly certain that Marlowe did not intend *calor* to be synonymous with either *choler* or the sanguine humour.[60]

Thus the *spirits*—common terms among the Elizabethans—were aeriform fluids of a celestial nature generated in the blood by natural heat (*calor*) and radical moisture (*humidum*). Acting as mediums which connected the liver, the heart, and the brain with the soul, the spirits served specifically the three special faculties of the soul as they coursed through the veins and arteries and gave to the body all its various activities. The soul, therefore, could not function properly in the exercise of its faculties (and thus give the body life and movement and understanding) unless the spirits were perfectly wrought and enjoyed an unobstructed passage through the veins and arteries. In particular, if the arteries became diseased or maladjusted in any way, neither the soul nor the body could benefit from the vital or animal spirits, and

---

the admirable qualities of the blood, . . . have feigned or imagined a spirit of celestial origin and nature; a body most subtile, attenuated, mobile, rapid, lucid, ethereal, participant in the qualities of the quintessence." *Ibid.,* pp. 502–503. Nor, of course, were Harvey's strictures against the prevailing theories concerning the *spirits, calidum innatum,* etc., immediately accepted, even by the physicians of the seventeenth century.

[58] Cf. La Primaudaye, *The French Academie* (London, 1594), p. 358, *et passim.*

[59] *Tamburlaine I,* iii.ii.69–71:

> I stand aghast; but most astonied
> To see his choler shut in secret thoughts,
> And wrapt in silence of his angry soul.

[60] Yet Professor Camden, *PQ,* viii (1929), 77, suggests, and Professor Battenhouse, *Marlowe's Tamburlaine,* p. 218, maintains, that *calor* is *choler;* and Miss Ellis-Fermor, *op. cit.,* pp. 273–274, states: *"humidum and calor:* moisture and warmth, presumably here in combination and therefore the sanguine humour."

the sick man thus afflicted had little chance for recovery. Indeed, as Tamburlaine's physician says,

> the soul,
> Wanting those organons by which it moves,
> Cannot endure, by argument of art.

We may now analyze more accurately the nature of Tamburlaine's malady. As a result of his intense passion (and, as I shall show anon, as a result of the position of his stars), Tamburlaine has occasioned in his body an excess of febrile heat. This "accidental heat" parches his arteries and dries up in his blood the radical moisture (*humidum*) which is necessary for the preservation of his natural heat (*calor*). The depletion of his *humidum* and *calor* (whose admixture in the blood gives rise to the *spirits*) prevents his soul's functions, stops his bodily activities, and thereby causes his death. Although Tamburlaine does not realize it, the more his passion is enraged the more malignant his bodily condition becomes, and the result is, of course, disastrous. Blindly, therefore, because of this "tragic flaw" in his character, Tamburlaine hurls himself onward to his death. The play is, from the Elizabethan point of view, therefore a tragedy of inordinate passions based somewhat painstakingly on sound Elizabethan psychological and physiological principles.

We have not completed our diagnosis of Tamburlaine's malady, however, until we ascertain what the stars have been doing while Tamburlaine suffered the throes of his agony. In more than half a dozen passages Marlowe calls attention to the fact that Tamburlaine's stars have ordained that he succeed.[61] At the time of Tamburlaine's illness, three of his soldiers plead with the stars to shed benevolent influences and overcome the malady which assails their leader. They plead in vain, for apparently the stellar powers forsake Tamburlaine at the very time when he needs them most. Possibly because the *calor* and the *spirits* are themselves identical with the essence of the stars, Tamburlaine's auspicious planets which have aided him so considerably heretofore are powerless to help him further. Possibly the same celestial force which made Tamburlaine's career heaven-ordained at last deals to him a kind of retributive justice in that the celestial bodily ingredients refuse to function properly. At any rate, to understand clearly

[61] See footnote 8.

what has happened in the heavens, we must proceed to the last item of
the physician's diagnosis—the critical days.

The physician has remarked significantly:

> Besides, my lord, this day is critical,
> Dangerous to those whose crisis is as yours:
>
> . . . . . . . . . . . . . .
>
> Yet, if your majesty may escape this day,
> No doubt but you shall soon recover all.

Critical days, the history of which goes back to Hippocrates and Galen,
were in general medical practice the days when the malignancy of a
disease was suddenly and swiftly altered for better or for worse—usually the seventh, fourteenth, twentieth, and twenty-seventh day after
decumbiture. Since "Galen and most of the ancient authorities believed
that critical days were influenced by the moon," [62] the mediaeval astrologers erected elaborate systems by which a disease could be diag-
nosed, attended, and healed according to the positions and influences
of the planets during these critical days. Wise mediaeval physicians
believed implicitly that any alteration of the qualities of a man's body
was dependent upon the stars; [63] Renaissance treatises on this subject
give abundant evidence that the tradition carried over into Elizabethan
times, and that many sixteenth-century doctors, living in the shadow
of mediaevalism, tempered their somewhat more orthodox medical
practices with astrological tenets. [64]

Arriving at the sick man's bedside, the physician who accepted these
iatromathematical doctrines would set about immediately to cast a
horoscope for the patient according to the hour or moment when the
poor man first experienced his distemper—just as Tamburlaine's physi-

[62] Francis Adams, op. cit., p. 198. Cf. Galen's De crisibus.

[63] Cf. W. C. Curry, Chaucer and the Mediaeval Sciences (New York, 1926),
ch. i.

[64] Cf. John Fage, Speculum Aegrotorum: The Sicke-mens Glasse (London,
1606); A Treatise of Mathematical Physick, Written by G. C. (appended to
Claudius Dariot's A Briefe Introduction to the Astrologicall Judgement of the
Starres, London, 1598); Nicholas Culpeper, Semeiotica Uranica: An Astrological
Judgement of Diseases from the Decumbiture of the Sick (London, 1674); Her-
mes Trismegistus, Iatromathematica, trans. by John Harvey (London, 1583);
L. Lemnius, The Secret Miracles of Nature, in Four Books, (London, 1628), Bk.
II, ch. 32, pp. 143 ff. Cf. also Lynn Thorndike. A History of Magic and Experi-
mental Science (New York, 1941), vols. v and vi, passim; and D. C. Allen, The
Star-Crossed Renaissance (Durham, N. C., 1941), Appendix, pp. 247-255.

cian seems to have done.[65] The position of the moon would indicate the time of the crisis, and principally the nature of her aspects with the other planets would indicate whether things would go well or no. Thus an astrologer-physician who was well acquainted with the technicalities of his business could tell as soon as he got his patient's horoscope cast just what positions the planets were in at decumbiture and would be in at any given time in the near future, and he could judge accordingly as to the sick man's chances for recovery. He might observe, for example, that at the decumbiture the moon was in opposition to Mars and squared with Saturn. Such a malefic configuration would bring about a dreadful illness indeed. But he might notice that when the critical day arrives the moon will have progressed to a point in the horoscope where she will be in conjunction with Jupiter and in trine aspect with Venus. This would be a favorable configuration, and the patient would doubtless recover. If, moreover, the physician should discover that a malignant configuration would exist on the critical day, but should notice that two days before that time the planetary aspects and positions will be favorable, he could bleed the patient (in the hour proper for phlebotomy), or administer the proper drugs, purgatives, cooling or hot drinks, and "comforters" of all sorts, by which he might be able to "break" the malady before the direful critical day arrives. Such was the method by which the astrologer-physician presaged as to his patient's illness and administered remedies accordingly; and such is the method that Tamburlaine's physician apparently pursued.

Assuming that unfavorable aspects of the planets on the critical day are in part responsible for Tamburlaine's illness, we may observe the astrological authorities to discover what stars might cause "accidental heat" in the veins or have an effect upon the body's *humidum* and *calor*. Doctor Robert Fludd, epitomizing in 1617 a host of past authorities, writes that Sol, Jupiter, and Mars are largely responsible for these "accidents" and qualities in the human body. Says he:

Sol, contrary to what some declare, ascribing to its dryness, is evidently hot [*calidum*] and . . . manifestly moist [*humidum*], if we consider its entire and exact composition; for, by an almost infallible demonstration, we have proved . . . that that solar mass is composed of equal portions of spiritual

[65] For the following discussion of astrological critical days, I have drawn indiscriminately upon all of the primary sources listed in note 64.

matter and of light. . . . But because formal light, heat forsooth, is said to have dominion in that body, which, entering into the composition of created things with its lucid substance, is called the innate heat of the living [*calidum viventis innatum*]; and because this thing . . . cannot move in the body apart from the vehicle, therefore this ray of the sun, a drop of the spiritual mass of the solar substance, . . . is that very familiar moisture . . . most friendly to the life of animals and vegetables, and is called the *humidum vitae radicale*. Hence the generative force of the sun is kindled, hence its multiplied strength and life, existing . . . from moisture regulated by such heat, . . . and acts effectively on this inferior world, and *by its actions arouses accidental heat* [*suisque actionibus calores accidentales escitare solet*].[66]

Sol has fluidity from innate heat [*calido innato*], and constant [fluidity] from radical moisture [*humido radicali*].[67]

Jupiter . . . makes heat and moisture [*Calidum & humidum*], in such a way, however, that moisture prevails.[68]

Mars is a planet composed of the fiery nature of Sol, but with less natural heat [*calore minus naturali*]. . . . Whence Mars has two evidences of heat, accidental [*per accidens*] and just so much from the nature of Sol, on account of its vicinity [near Sol in the heavens]. By reason of its accidental heat [*caloris sui accidentalis*] it is thus malicious and destructive in its nature; . . . Hence the rising of bile and biliousness.[69]

Thus Mars, because of his dryness and heat, might debilitate the *humidum;* and Saturn, because of his cold, dry, malignant qualities, might diminish the *calor;* for Fludd reports further:

Saturn rules the East, because, although that part of the day is by nature warm [*calida*], on account of the coldness of Saturn, that heat [*caliditas*] is, in a certain manner, said [to be] moderated.[70] . . . Saturn in a square aspect with Sol diminishes the heat [*caliditatem*] somewhat.[71]

Thus Mars or Sol might have occasioned the "accidental heat" that parched the frenzied despot's veins, and any malignant aspect between Sol and Saturn, or Jupiter and Saturn, or Mars and Sol, or Mars and Jupiter, might have caused the depletion of the vital *humidum* and *calor* in Tamburlaine's heat-ridden body.

[66] *Utriusque Cosmi Maioris scilicet et Minoris Metaphysica, Physica atque Technica Historia in duo Volumina secundum Cosmi differentam divisa* (Opphemi, 1617–1618), II, 653–654. For the original Latin of these passages, see *PMLA*, LIX (1944), 713, where this chapter first appeared.

[67] *Ibid.*, 657.       [68] *Ibid.*, 646.       [69] *Ibid.*, p. 648.       [70] *Ibid.*, p. 637.

[71] *Ibid.*, p. 699.

Marlowe, however, has mentioned none of these specific configurations; nor has he given us sufficient information by which we might cast Tamburlaine's horoscope, actually determine (as his physician evidently did) the exact status of the heavens during Tamburlaine's illness, and speculate upon his chances for recovery during the critical day. Undoubtedly an Elizabethan audience understood by what means these speculations were ascertainable. Possibly the very mention of "critical day" would suffice to convey the playwright's meaning—as would, say, "appendectomy" for us today. At any rate, Marlowe—possibly to avoid being obvious—left entirely to his audience's imagination the specific planets which were woefully aspected when the accidental febrile heat dried up Tamburlaine's blood, parched his veins, and so debilitated his *humidum* and *calor* that he was speedily dispatched.

We have, therefore, a direct and an indirect cause for Tamburlaine's decease: his passion and his stars. His malady, involving a portion of his body comparable to and influenced by the essence of the celestial bodies, is initiated by his innate passion; but his illness occurs at a time when the stars, previously favorable to his fortunes, are in some way conspiring against his state. His catastrophe is, therefore, precipitated not only by the "tragic flaw" in his character but also by his astral destiny.[72]

[72] The materials in this chapter were first published in *PMLA*, LIX (1944), 696–714.

## CHAPTER TWO

# FOOLISH MYCETES' UNFORTUNATE HOROSCOPE

WITH THE POSSIBLE EXCEPTION of Bajazeth, Tamburlaine's chief adversary, none of the minor characters who give vitality to Marlowe's *Tamburlaine,* Part I, are distinguished or even characterized in the several accounts which Marlowe used as sources.[1] Because of this meagerness of raw materials, Marlowe was compelled to fall back upon his originality in making the minor characters distinct.[2] In doing so he characterized Mycetes, King of Persia, as so utterly absurd that he might be classed with that group of dramatic simpletons headed by Sir Andrew Aguecheek. Mycetes is nevertheless the first obstacle in Tamburlaine's path of conquest, is therefore essential to Tamburlaine's rise, and (as one critic of the play has remarked) "remains one of the few humorous characters in Elizabethan drama intrinsic to the central story yet subordinate to it." [3] The following discussion presents a neglected aspect of Marlowe's characterization of this silly old king; or, specifically, shows how by means of astrology Marlowe has vitalized the character of Mycetes—and incidentally the character of Cosroe also.

The play opens with the following dialogue between Mycetes and his brother, Cosroe, who is envious that such a stupid man as Mycetes wears the crown:

> *Mycetes:*  Brother Cosroe, I find myself agriev'd;
> Yet insufficient to express the same,

[1] The principal sources for *Tamburlaine* are pointed out in Una M. Ellis-Fermor's edition of the play, *Tamburlaine the Great* (London, 1930), pp. 17–61; and in Thomas C. Izard's "The Principal Source of Marlowe's *Tamburlaine,*" *MLN,* LVIII (1943), 411–417. See also Leslie Spence, "The Influence of Marlowe's Sources on *Tamburlaine I,*" *MP,* XXIV (1926), 181–199, and "Tamburlaine and Marlowe," *PMLA,* XLII (1927), 604–622.

[2] That Marlowe has done this has been adequately shown by Miss Spence in her two papers cited above.

[3] Spence, *op. cit.,* p. 191.

> For it requires a great and thundering speech:
> Good brother, tell the cause unto my lords;
> I know you have a better wit than I.
>
> *Cosroe:*  Unhappy Persia, that in former age
> Hast been the seat of mighty conquerors,
> That, in their prowess and their policies,
> Have triumphed over Afric, and the bounds
> Of Europe, . . .
> Now to be ruled and governed by a man
> At whose birthday Cynthia with Saturn joined,
> And Jove, the Sun, and Mercury denied
> To shed their influence in his fickle brain!
> Now Turks and Tartars shake their swords at thee,
> Meaning to mangle all thy provinces.
>
> *Mycetes:*  Brother, I see your meaning well enough,
> And through your planets I perceive you think
> I am not wise enough to be a king:
> But I refer me to my noblemen,
> That know my wit, and can be witnesses.[4]

In addition to presenting us with a portion of the Persian potentate's horoscope and marking Cosroe as an adept of astrology, this passage indicates that Mycetes is (especially in Cosroe's opinion) not only an unfortunate ruler but also somewhat a fool. As the play progresses, Cosroe continually calls attention to Mycetes' lack of prepossessing mental qualities: he refers to Mycetes' lack of wisdom, to "the folly of their king," to "the witless king," to the "foolish king," to Mycetes' "weary witless head," and to "My witless brother."[5] Tamburlaine himself speaks of Mycetes as "the fool," and first accosts him in battle by flinging at him the derisive interrogation, "Are you the witty king of Persia?"[6] Anyone who reads Scene iv of Act II, wherein Tamburlaine snatches the Persian crown from Mycetes, who has attempted (of all things!) to hide it in a hole, cannot doubt that the Persian potentate

[4] *Tamburlaine the Great,* ed. U. M. Ellis-Fermor (London, 1930), i.i.1–22. On the astrological allusion in this passage, Miss Fermor comments: "Here his astrological references are general rather than technical. I imagine the moon's share in the make-up of Mycetes to have been giddy variableness and Saturn's dull heaviness of mind, while the beneficence of Jupiter, the geniality of Sol and the keen-mindedness of Mercury were denied."

[5] *Ibid.,* i.i.92, 97; ii.i.64; ii.iii.62; ii.i.46; ii.v.42.

[6] *Ibid.,* ii.iii.46. and ii.iv.22.

is, as Cosroe maintains, an utterly silly and witless fool. At any rate, he is unquestionably an incapable, thoughtless, timorous ruler who allows his kingdom to go to seed unrestrained. He has long complained of Tamburlaine's "incivil outrages" and highway robberies inflicted upon Persian merchants; yet he has made no preparations whatever to check this "Scythian thief" whose intentions to make himself sole monarch of Asia are widely known.[7] The neighboring nations "sit and laugh to scorn" Mycetes' "regiment,"[8] and the Babylonians are on the point of revolting "from Persian government, / Unless they have a wiser king" than Mycetes.[9] When Cosroe tells Mycetes of these threats to the Persian government, the king merely whines that by Cosroe's "contemptuous words" he is "abus'd," and feebly swears revenge "by my royal seat . . . / Embossed with silk."[10] His reign has been so unsuccessful, or so unwise, that his specially trusted forces under Theridamas desert;[11] the idle Persian troops, unpaid and undisciplined, "threaten civil war, / And openly exclaim against the king";[12] and Cosroe, the Persian noblemen, and the governors of outlying Persian districts finally plot against Mycetes and tyrannically set up Cosroe as their monarch.[13] The last we hear of Mycetes is that he has been routed by Tamburlaine's forces and has "yielded to the stroke of war."[14]

Failing to believe that the astrological allusion in the opening lines of *Tamburlaine* is merely a digressive element of the play or a typical example of Elizabethan clap-trap, and strongly suspecting that Marlowe had some purpose in deliberately inserting it there, I should like to examine the Renaissance astrological authorities to determine just what this particular configuration means, and to see if the stars— which Marlowe has mentioned with apparent care—have anything to do with the Persian king's mental weakness and political misfortunes.

We are told that in the figure representing the heavens at the time of Mycetes' birth Saturn was in conjunction with the moon, and that three other planets (Jupiter, Sol, and Mercury) were so posited as to have had no effect upon Mycetes' mental faculties. Now Saturn was considered by the astrologers to be the most powerful of the malefic planets. He worked havoc when in dominion over any of the other

[7] *Ibid.*, I.i.30–43.                  [8] *Ibid.*, I.i.117.                  [9] *Ibid.*, I.i.90–92.
[10] *Ibid.*, I.i.97–106.            [11] *Ibid.*, I.ii.152–250.            [12] *Ibid.*, I.i.140–150.
[13] *Ibid.*, I.i.110–188.          [14] *Ibid.*, II.v.12.

planets, and was on most occasions envious, covetous, jealous, a malicious dissembler, a servant of anger, a begetter of strife, a spreader of incurable diseases, an accomplisher of destruction and decay.[15] Luna was almost equally powerful, some astrologers ascribing to her more influence than to any other planet on a person's health, physical make-up, and sensual faculties.[16] At any rate, all the astrologers are agreed that any planet exerts a malevolent influence when in corporal conjunction with either of the malefics (i.e., Saturn or Mars), and that a conjunction of Saturn and Luna is a most malignant configuration. Augier Ferrier, in his widely-circulated Renaissance textbook of astrology, remarks: "Unfortune are the planets when they be joined with Saturne or with Mars, or when they receive evil aspects of them."[17] Jovianus Pontanus, an eminent sixteenth-century writer of philosophical and astrological texts, tells us: "If the Moon be in conjunction or opposition at the birth time with the Sun, Saturn, or Mars . . . the head and brain is like to be misaffected with pernicious humours, to be melancholy, lunatic, or mad."[18] The 19th and 77th Aphorisms of Jerome Cardan, one of the Renaissance's most renowned astrologers, are especially pertinent:

19. The Moon full of light in conjunction with Mars, makes the Native to be counted a fool; but if she be void of light and with Saturn, he is so indeed.

[15] Cf. Claudius Ptolemy, *Tetrabiblos or Quadripartitum,* trans. J. M. Ashmand (London, 1822; Chicago, 1936), Bk. II, ch. ix and Bk. III, ch. xviii; Alchabitius, *Libellus ysagogicus* (Venetiis, 1591), sig. bb3v; Albumasar, *De magnis coniunctionibus annorum revolutionibus* (Venetiis, 1489), sig. h3; Albohazen Haly filius Abenragel, *Libri de iudiciis astrorum* (Basileae, 1531), p. 9; Guido Bonatus, *Tractatus astrologicus* (Venetiis, 1491), Pars IIII, cap. lxiii.

[16] Cf. Ptolemy, *op. cit.,* Bk. III, chs. xviii, xix. To the astrologer-physician, Luna was virtually the most important planet in the horoscope, the malignancy of the patient's disease depending largely upon the moon's aspects with Saturn or Mars. Cf. Hermes Trismegistus, *Iatromathematica,* trans. John Harvey (London, 1583), pp. 12 ff.; John Fage, *Speculum Aegrotorum: The Sicke-mens Glasse* (London, 1606), *passim; A Treatise of Mathematical Physick, Written by G. C.* (appended to Claudius Dariot's *A Briefe Introduction to the Astrologicall Iudgement of the Starres,* trans. Fabian Withers, London, 1598), sig. H, *et passim.*

[17] *An Astronomical Discourse of the Judgement of Nativities,* trans. Thomas Kelway (London, 1593), p. 7. Cf. also Claudius Dariot, *op. cit.,* Ch. x: "Luna, being in her decrease with Saturne, is unfortunate."

[18] Cited by Robert Burton, *The Anatomy of Melancholy,* Part I, Section 2.

77. When the Moon is joined to Saturn in an Angle, the Native, though a grandee, will be reduced to poverty.[19]

John Baptista Porta, a scholarly student of celestial physiognomy who records faithfully the opinions of Albohazen Haly and other astrological authorities, reports:

If Saturn is joined with Luna, and is badly posited, the native shall be deformed, silly, stinking, fearful, vile-faced, . . . Haly says: Saturn with Luna, badly posited, makes the native unseemly, weak in mind and character, of so little judgment that nothing in himself is esteemed, or recognized, or even considered.[20]

And William Lilly, England's foremost astrologer of the seventeenth century, who garnered his material from his predecessors, regards the conjunction of Saturn and Luna thus:

If Saturn be significator, the person is restless and unsettled in his purposes. He is not very fortunate. If Luna be significator, he is . . . miserable and dejected, of unpleasant manners and sullen disposition; . . . . He frequently commits the most unaccountable errors in affairs of the greatest consequence; as, through excess of prudence, he is very likely to doubt and deliberate in the moment of action.[21]

It would seem, therefore, that the astrological authorities were agreed upon the vitiating influence of a conjunction between Saturn and Luna, and that this conjunction might be blamed especially for endowing one with weak mental faculties and effecting for one considerable misfortune.

According to Marlowe's brief portrait of Mycetes, this Persian potentate is possessed with just the sort of characteristics that this configuration in his natal horoscope presages. He is ridiculously silly, given to all kinds of folly, and possessed of a brain certainly in some manner grievously "misaffected." Because he is so unsettled in his purposes, he is beset with hindrances on every side; because of his unwarranted deliberations in moments when he should act vigorously, he commits

---

[19] *Anima Astrologiae, . . . together with the Choicest Aphorisms of the Seven Segments of Jerome Cardan of Milan, Edited by William Lilly* (London, 1675, 1886), pp. 79, 85. The "angles" are the first, fourth, seventh, and tenth houses of a horoscope; see figure on p. 105.

[20] *Physiognomoniae Coelestis Libri Sex* (Rothomagi, 1603, 1650), pp. 66–67.

[21] *Christian Astrology* (London, 1647). I quote from a recent reprint, edited by Zadkiel, entitled *An Introduction to Astrology* (London, 1939), p. 318.

inexcusable errors in his affairs of state. Anyone with knowledge of and faith in astrology would point unhesitatingly to Mycetes' weak mentality and vacillating activities as being a result of the malignant conjunction of Saturn and Luna in his natal horoscope. Cosroe accordingly considers himself justified in believing that Mycetes would remain forever a fool; and therefore refuses, finally, to tolerate his rule longer.

Cosroe has remarked that Jupiter, Sol, and Mercury failed to shed influences on Mycetes' mind doubtless because these planets in particular could have given Mycetes wit and eloquence and made him a skilful, magnanimous, and successful ruler. Jupiter, the most powerful of the benefic planets, if posited fortunately in Mycetes' horoscope, would have mitigated more than any other planet the evil influence of a malignant conjunction—even one of Saturn and the moon. For Albohazen Haly says:

Jupiter abhors Saturn and his nature, prohibits and restrains him in all his works. The former teaches and fosters goodness, . . . and governs whatever is commodious or agreeable. He is . . . fortunate in all his activities and influences, loving councils of wise men, just ordinances, and discriminating judgments.[22]

And (Albohazen Haly continues) when Jupiter is the sole lord of the horoscope and posited fortunately,

he makes the native of great nobility of mind, honorable, . . . of fine reputation, just, . . . gentle of disposition, quiet, unruffled, eschewing vain things; such a person . . . meditates and plans good actions, . . . is diligent and well-doing, and knows how to guard, serve, and retain friends.[23]

Jupiter's influence on the mental qualities is reported thus by astrology's chief spokesman, Claudius Ptolemy:

When Jupiter alone has dominion of the mind, and is gloriously situated, he renders it generous, gracious, pious, reverent, joyous, courteous, lofty, liberal, just, magnanimous, noble, self-acting, compassionate, fond of learning, beneficent, benevolent, and calculated for government.[24]

Thus Jupiter's influence might have endowed Mycetes with an extremely laudible nativity and made him a venerated king. Influences

---

[22] *Libri de iudiciis astrorum* (Basileae, 1551), p. 10.
[23] *Ibid.,* p. 169.    [24] *Op. cit.,* Bk. iii, ch. xviii.

from Sol might also have wrought for Mycetes a more substantial mind and character, for Ptolemy continues:

The Sun, when conciliated with the lord of the mental temperament, and in a glorious position, increases probity, industry, honour, and all laudable qualities.[25]

William Lilly writes thus of a man whose horoscope is dominated by Sol:

He is . . . of incomparable judgment; of great majesty and stateliness, . . . The solar man usually speaks with gravity, but not many words, and these with great confidence and command. . . .[26]

The lack of Sol's influence, then, explains in part why Mycetes is incapable of "a great and thundering speech." Concerning Mercury's influence on the mentality, Ptolemy says:

Mercury, alone having dominion of the mind, and being in a glorious position, renders it prudent, clever, sensible, capable of great learning, inventive, expert, logical, studious of nature, speculative, of good genius, emulous, benevolent, skilful in argument, accurate in conjecture, adapted to sciences and mysteries, and tractable.[27]

Lilly reports similar qualities:

Being well-dignified, Mercury represents a man of a subtle and political brain and intellect, an excellent disputant or logician, arguing with learning and discretion, and using much eloquence in his speech; . . . sharp and witty, learning almost anything without a teacher; ambitious of being exquisite in every science, . . . a man of unwearied fancy, . . . able by his own genius to produce wonders, . . .[28]

Mercury, then, favorably posited, would have made Mycetes a wise, eloquent, and clever man. But such prognostications as these show only what Mycetes' character and fortunes might have been. Cosroe can anticipate for his erring brother none of these beneficent influences, for he knows definitely that Jupiter, Sol, and Mercury "denied / To shed their influence in his fickle brain!" Cosroe, being well-versed in astrological lore, therefore provided himself with a splendid motive for his contempt and for his revolt.

It is not unreasonable to suppose that Marlowe ascertained from some reliable source the influence of the particular configuration he

[25] Loc. cit.                                        [26] Op. cit., p. 43. Cf. also Porta, op. cit., p. 42.
[27] Op. cit., Bk. III, ch. xviii.                   [28] Op. cit., p. 48.

described in Mycetes' horoscope; and that he fully intended to draw this ridiculous king's character—particularly in the mind's eye of Cosroe—in accordance with the technicalities laid down by the astrological authorities. In any case, it seems to me that Marlowe has endowed these two minor characters with a certain vitality and distinctiveness by including in his portrayal of them this little touch of astrological learning; and that to a discerning Elizabethan audience, who attached considerable importance to the tenets of astrology, this "scientific" verisimilitude must have been particularly artistic and effective.[29]

[29] The materials in this chapter were published as "The Horoscope of Mycetes in Marlowe's *Tamburlaine I*," *PQ*, xxv (1946), 371–377.

## CHAPTER THREE

# ASTROLOGICAL "CHARACTERS" IN DOCTOR FAUSTUS' MAGIC CIRCLE

WHEN CHRISTOPHER MARLOWE'S Doctor Faustus decides that his studies in philosophy, law, physic, and divinity are odious, petty, and contemptible, he becomes "ravished" with a desire for magical knowledge. To prepare himself for the practice of magic and various necromantic skills, Faustus turns not only to books of occult lore but also to works of astrology. His friends, Valdes and Cornelius, who have continually reminded him of all the wonders he can accomplish should he know how to raise spirits, inform him that astrology must be one of the bases of his study. Cornelius explains to him:

> He that is grounded in astrology,
> Enriched with tongues, well seen in minerals,
> Hath all the principles magic doth require.
>
> (i.i.139–141) [1]

Marlowe found the astrological proclivities of Faustus stated in the primary source of his play, the English *Faustbook,* wherein we read:

Faustus accompanied himselfe with divers that were seen [2] in the divilish Arts, and that had the *Chaldean, Persian, Hebrew, Arabian,* and *Greeke* tongues, using Figures, Characters, Conjurations, Incantations, with many other ceremonies belonging to the infernal Arts, . . . in so much that hee . . . waxed a worldly man, and named himselfe an Astrologian, and a Mathematician: & . . . sometimes a Phisistian. [3]

The *Faustbook* as well as the Doctor's friendly advisers are entirely

---

[1] I cite throughout from *The Tragical History of Doctor Faustus,* ed. Frederick S. Boas (New York, 1932).

[2] seen: *versed in.* Notice the same word in the previous quotation.

[3] *The Historie of the Damnable Life, and deserved death of Doctor John Faustus* (London, 1592), ch. i, p. 2; reprinted by P. M. Palmer and R. P. Moore, *The Sources of the Faust Tradition* (New York, 1936), p. 136.

correct from the Renaissance point of view, for in proclaiming astrology a requisite of magic they are supported by perhaps the most renowned occultist of the sixteenth century: Henry Cornelius Agrippa. In Agrippa's *De occulta philosophia* we find two pertinent statements:

Of all operations in occult science there is not one that is not rooted in astrology.[4]

Whosoever is desirous to study in this Faculty [i.e., Magic], if he be not skilled in Natural Philosophy, . . . in the Mathematics, and in the Aspects and Figures of the Stars, upon which depends the sublime virtue and property of every thing: and if he be not learned in Theology, . . . he cannot be possibly able to understand the rationality of Magic. For there is no work that is done by mere Magic . . . that doth not comprehend these three Faculties.[5]

If he is to be a competent magician, Faustus must therefore acquire— among other things—some knowledge of astrology.

The play has not progressed very far before Faustus feels capable of raising spirits in the manner of an expert conjurer. He draws a magic circle and proceeds to test his newly acquired abilities, saying:

> Faustus, begin thine incantations,
> And try if devils will obey thy hest,
> Seeing thou hast prayed and sacrificed to them.
> Within this circle is Jehovah's name,
> Forward and backward anagrammatized,
> The breviated names of holy saints,
> Figures of every adjunct to the Heavens,
> And characters of signs and erring stars,
> By which the spirits are enforced to rise:
> Then fear not, Faustus, but be resolute,
> And try the utmost magic can perform.
> (1.iii.5–15)

The Latin incantations which follow bring forth Mephistophilis, and Faustus, taken aback at first, finally exults:

---

[4] Henry Morley, *The Life of Henry Cornelius Agrippa* (London, 1856), I, 184. Morley's *Life* contains a translation of Agrippa's *De occulta philosophia*, the passage cited being from Bk. II, ch. liii.

[5] Henry Cornelius Agrippa von Nettesheim, *Three Books of Occult Philosophy or Magic*, trans. J. F. (London, 1651); partly reprinted and edited by Willis F. Whitehead (New York, 1897), Bk. I, ch. ii, pp. 37–38.

> Such is the force and magic of my spells:
> Now Faustus, thou art conjuror laureat,
> That canst command great Mephistophilis.
>                                            (1.iii.33–35)

It will be noticed that in the process of his conjuration Faustus has recourse not only to incantations, prayers, sacrifices, and theological names, but also to astrology. The writings of the mediaevalists Thomas Aquinas and Roger Bacon [6] show that Faustus proceeded properly. Bacon scornfully commented that magicians "invoke demons . . . by the idlest sort of circles, figures, and characters, and by the stupidest incantations and unreasonable prayers in which they put their trust." [7] Aquinas pointed out that all magicians "employ invocations, . . . figures and characters, sacrifices, . . . constellations," and that "as a result, apparitions of rational beings are summoned and answer questions." [8] Into his magic circle, therefore, through which he shall raise spirits, Faustus has cast certain *characters* of the signs and planets. For a full explanation of these magical *characters* of the stars, we may turn again to Agrippa's *De occulta philosophia*.

Agrippa rehearses the mediaeval occultists in basing all magical philosophy on the commonplace generalization that everything inferior (i.e., of the earth) is subject to and governed by things superior (i.e., of the heavens). [9] He informs us specifically that not only the body, actions, and dispositions of man but also all stones, metals, plants, animals, and places are under the influence of one or more of the planets, the signs of the zodiac, and the fixed stars. [10] All things on earth (says Agrippa) are solary, lunary, jovial, saturnine, martial, venerian, or mercurial, according to the nature of the strong impressions that are communicated by the rays of a particular planet. For example, Jupiter governs the air, man's abdomen, ribs, blood, Spirit of Life, increase and nourishment; tin, silver, gold, beryl, sapphire, emerald, hyacinth; henbane, violet, mint, basil, mace; poplar trees, oaks, beech, holly, hazel, ash, dogwood; sugar, raisins, barley, wheat;

---

[6] Bacon is one of the authors which Marlowe says Faustus read (1.i.55).

[7] Cited from Lynn Thorndike, *A History of Magic and Experimental Science* (New York, 1923), II, 669.

[8] *Ibid.*, II, 603.                          [9] Whitehead edition, Bk. I, ch. i, pp. 33–34.

[10] *Ibid.*, Bk. I, chs. xxii, xxxi, xxxiv.

elephants, harts, sheep, lambs, hens, egg-yolk, cuckoos, storks, pelicans, eagles, dolphins, anchovies; Spain, Arabia; tribunals, schools, and so on.[11] Similar government is assigned to each of the other planets, the signs of the zodiac, and the fixed stars.[12]

Now each of the planets, having its peculiar nature and property, is possessed of a *seal* or *character* which (through stellar rays) it impresses on inferior things subject to it. Such *characters* appear especially in plants, trees, stones, and members of animals.[13] For example, the roots of certain plants, the bones and members of certain animals, the joints and knots of certain trees influenced by Jupiter will show, when cut, the *characters* of that planet. Agrippa states the doctrine clearly:

All Stars have their peculiar natures, properties, and conditions, the Seals and Characters whereof they produce, through their rays, even in these inferior things, viz., in elements, in stones, in plants, in animals, and their members; whence every natural thing receives, from a harmonious disposition and from its star shining upon it, some particular Seal, or Character, stamped upon it; which Seal or Character is the significator of that Star, or harmonious disposition containing in it a peculiar Virtue. . . . Everything, therefore, hath its character pressed upon it by its star for some particular effect, especially by that star which doth principally govern it. And these Characters contain and retain in them the peculiar Natures, Virtues, and Roots of their Stars, and produce the like operations upon other things, on which they are reflected. . . . Ancient Wise Men . . . did set down in writings the Images of the Stars, their Figures, Seals, Marks, Characters, such as Nature herself did describe, by the rays of the Stars, in these inferior bodies—some in stones, some in plants, and joints and knots of boughs, and some in divers members of animals. For the bay-tree and the marigold are Solary Plants, and in their roots and knots, being cut off, shew the Characters of the Sun. So also in the bones and shoulder-blades in animals; . . . and in stones and stony things the Characters and Images of celestial things are often found. . . . We shall here note some few Seals and Characters of the Planets, such as the ancient chiromancers knew of in the hands of men.[14]

And therewith Agrippa obligingly records for us a set of these Characters, as follows:[15]

---

[11] *Ibid.*, Bk. i, chs. xxiv, xxx, xxxi, xlviii.      [12] *Ibid.*, Bk. i, ch. xxxii.

[13] One is reminded of the "Gall of goat, slips of yew" which go into the Witches' cauldron in *Macbeth,* iv.i.27.

[14] *Ibid.*, Bk. i, ch. xxxiii.

[15] Reproduced from the 1533 edition of *De occulta philosophia,* pp. xxxix–xl, Henry E. Huntington Library copy. Cf. Morley, *op. cit.,* i, 138.

SEQVVNTVR FIGVRAE LITERARVM
DIVINARVM.
Literæ fiue charaĉteres Saturni.

ⵣ ⵜ ⵏⵡⵉⵅⴺⵯ

Literæ feu charaĉteres Iouis.

ⵯⴺⵇⵜⵅⵎⵉⵜⵜ ⴸ ⵏⵉ

Literæ feu charaĉteres Martis.

ⵏⴷⵜⵜ ⵒ ⵛⵉⵇ

Literæ fiue charaĉteres Solis.

ⵒ ⴸⵉⵜⵏⵗⵉⵉⵉⵡⵉⵏ

Literæ fiue charaĉteres Veneris.

ⵏⵜ ⵑ ⴸ ⴺ

Literæ fiue charaĉteres Mercurii.

ⵯⵯ ⵗⴺⵯⵉ ⵏⵉⵑ

Literæ fiue charaĉteres Lunæ.

ⵉ ⴷ ⵯⵯ ⵗ ⵏⴸ

Such *characters,* as Agrippa has told us, emit rays having the peculiar virtue which has been impressed upon them by the star whence
they proceed, and thus can operate upon things on which they are
reflected. Magical experimenters engraved them on metals or precious
stones, or moulded them in wax or gum; and then with the aid of
these and much hocus-pocus proceeded to promote or dispell lust, discord, disease, wealth, love, homicide, and the like.[16] At any rate, should
one desire to receive "virtue" from a particular star, he could bring
himself under its influence by the employment of those things upon
which that star's *character* is stamped.

These, then, are the *characters* of the signs and "erring stars" (or
planets) which Doctor Faustus employs, with other occult elements
and manifestations, to conjure up the spirit of Mephistophilis. And it
is quite right that Faustus should use them thus in raising up either
good or evil spirits, for Agrippa says:

Magicians teach that celestial gifts may . . . be drawn down by opportune
influences of the heaven; and so, also, by these celestial gifts, the celestial

---

[16] Cf. Thorndike, *op. cit.,* I, 645; II, 820–21; IV, 171, 279, 295.

angels (as they are servants of the stars) may be procured and conveyed to us, . . . according to the rules of natural philosophy and astronomy.[17]

No man is ignorant that evil spirits, by evil and profane arts, may be raised up, . . . that the gods of the world may be raised by us, or, at least, the ministering spirits, or servants of these gods, as Mercurius saith.[18]

Marlowe does not tell us which star or planet governed the *characters* in the magic circle through which he called up Mephistophilis. But if Faustus is to make any pretense toward being a magician of the sixteenth century, Marlowe had to provide him with skill in astrology and by all means throw into his magic circle some *characters* of the planets.[19]

[17] Whitehead edition, Bk. 1, ch. xxxviii.

[18] *Ibid.,* Bk. 1, ch. xxxix.

[19] It is interesting to note the sport that Mercutio makes of the magic circle a few years later in *Romeo and Juliet,* ii.i.6–29. Cf. also Paul H. Kocher, "The Witchcraft Basis in Marlowe's *Faustus,*" *MP,* xxxviii (1940), 9–36, esp. 19–20.

# CHAPTER FOUR

# ASTROLOGY MOTIVATES
## A COMEDY

THE COURTLY CIRCLE of Elizabethan theatre-goers probably took exceptional notice when John Lyly personified the seven planets and employed them as the *modus operandi* of his comedy *The Woman in the Moone*.[1] For this was indeed a novel idea. Not since Robert Henryson's pictorial representations of the seven planets sitting in judgment on the fate of Cresseid in *The Testament of Cresseid* (ca. 1460?) had anyone given in a piece of literature so large a role to the planets. In using them to motivate the entire plot of his play, Lyly's employment of them was unique and no doubt entertaining.

In Lyly's play the shepherds of Utopia petition Nature to create for them a woman comrade, and Nature endows her creation, Pandora, with all the excellencies of the gods and goddesses in heaven. The seven planets, however, are envious because they have not been consulted in Pandora's creation, and accordingly determine to work her ruin. Each of the planets in turn attempts to bring about Pandora's undoing by subjecting her to its particular influence. Thereupon all of Pandora's actions and relations with the shepherds, caused by these planetary influences, form the simple plot of Lyly's play.

Naturally it is for dramatic purposes that Lyly personifies the planets. But all of the Mediaeval and Renaissance astrologers likewise write of the planets as animate beings; the texts of Albumasar, John Sadeler, and others contain dozens of woodcuts illustrating the persons of Sol, Saturn, Luna, *et al.* riding across the heavens in chariots.[2] They did

---

[1] *The Complete Works of John Lyly,* ed. R. W. Bond (Oxford, 1902), vol. III. I cite throughout from this edition.

[2] Albumasar, *Introductorium in astronomiam* (Augsburg, 1489), and *De magnis conjunctionibus* (Augsburg, 1489); Jan. Sadeler, *Planetarum effectus et eorum in signis zodiaci super provincias, regiones, et civitates dominia* (Antwerp, 1585).

not treat the planets exclusively as astronomical bodies in the heavens, and Lyly's idea of personifying them is therefore well-authenticated.

The powers or influences which the astrologers assigned to each of the seven planets depended upon the planet's *position* in the heavens and its relation there to the signs of the zodiac and the other planets. The generally evil planet Saturn could, under certain conditions, be benevolent; and the usually benefic planet Venus could in similar manner be malefic—depending upon the planet's position and upon other planets aspecting it.[3] Lyly does not tell us precisely what astrological position the planets in his play assume, the stage-direction in the Quarto stating merely that the planets "Ascend" (no doubt to a dias on the stage) and the text itself informing us that they "signorize awhile."[4] They make their appearance in the play according to astrological order: i.e., Saturn, Jupiter, Mars, Sol, Venus, Mercury, Luna.

When Saturn "Ascends" to "signorize awhile" over Pandora, he says:

> I shall instill such melancholy moode,
> As by corrupting of her purest blood,
> Shall first with sullen sorrowes clowde her braine,
> And then surround her heart with froward care:
> She shall be sick with passions of the heart,
> Selfwild, and toungtide, but full fraught with teares.
>
> (1.i.144–149)

Pandora then finds that she is "unfit for company," that "swelling clowdes overcast her braine," that "fretful sorrow captivates her tongue," and that she "had rather choose to weep then speak her mind."[5] When Stesias kisses her hand in admiration, she discourteously hits him in the mouth. She frowns and will not speak. When the shepherds play music to cure her melancholy, she runs away.[6]

Saturn's power for causing melancholy, sullen sorrows, froward

---

[3] If, for example, the generally evil planet Saturn were in the sign of Capricorn or of Aquarius, the astrologer could presage profound knowledge, love of noblemen, credit and great riches, and advancement over all one's brethren. If the extremely benefic planet Jupiter were in these signs, the astrologer must presage at best little courage and general poverty. Cf. Augier Ferrier, *A Learned Astronomical Discourse of the Judgement of Nativities,* trans. Thomas Kelway (London, 1593), sig. 12v.

[4] *The Woman in the Moone,* 1.ii.135, 138.

[5] 1.i.156–160, 171–176.     [6] 1.i.180–222.

cares, and for making one solitary, tongue-tied, silent, self-willed, and weepy is well-authenticated by the astrologers. Alchabitius explains:

Saturn is evil, . . . produces and fosters . . . men of melancholic complexion. He signifies . . . profound silence, . . . mistrust and suspicion, moving men to complaints and mutterings.[7]

Augier Ferrier points out that Saturn makes one

sadde, solitarie, fearful, melancholie, faint-hearted, . . . rejecting the counsell of others; fearing that all the world doth deceive him; uncivil, . . . flying the company of men unlesse it be to deceive them.[8]

Henry Cornelius Agrippa writes:

The gestures and motions of . . . Saturn . . . are . . . beating of the breast or striking of the head; . . . bowing of the knee, and a fixed look downwards, as of one praying; also weeping, and such like.[9]

Claudius Ptolemy says:

Saturn . . . will make men . . . ill-disposed, . . . fond of solitude, . . . void of natural affection.[10]

And William Lilly writes that Saturn in the sign of Gemini "signifies diseases proceeding from bad blood," and that Saturn in Virgo or in Aries "shews the blood corrupted." [11] Thus substantiated are the characteristics employed by Lyly peculiar to Saturn's influence: melancholy, sullenness, silence, sorrow, frowning, weeping, and incivility. Though he is correct in saying that Saturn corrupts the blood, he is wrong in assigning to Saturn "passions of the heart"; for none of the astrologers

[7] *Libellus Isagogicus Abdilazi . . . qui dictur Alchabitius* (Venice, 1491), sig. bb3v.

[8] *Op. cit.,* p. 13.

[9] *Three Books of Occult Philosophy or Magic,* trans. J. F. (London, 1651), Bk. I, ch. 52; cited from W. F. Whitehead's reproduction of J. F's translation (New York, 1897), pp. 156–157.

[10] *Quadripartitum,* Bk. III, ch. xviii; cited from J. M. Ashmand's translation (London, 1822), reprinted (Chicago, 1936), p. 109.

[11] *Christian Astrology* (London, 1647); cited from Zadkiel's 1852 edition entitled *An Introduction to Astrology by William Lilly* (London, 1939), pp. 35–36. See, in addition to authorities cited above, Albumasar, *De magnis conjunctionibus* (Venice, 1489), sig. h3; Albohazen Haly filius Abenragel, *Libri de judiciis astrorum* (Basle, 1531), p. 9; Bartholomaeus Anglicus, *De proprietatibus rerum* (Venice, 1483), lib. VIII, cap. xxiii; Guido Bonatus, *De astronomia tractatus X* (Basle, 1550), Pars. IIII, cap. lxiii.

give this jurisdiction to Saturn, and Hermes Trismegistus states definitely that "all passions of the heart . . . proceed from the Sun and Mars."[12] But Lyly, we must conclude, has with general accuracy used Saturnine characteristics that might be found in any number of astrological textbooks.

Jupiter, the next planet to ascend, says:

> Now Jupiter shall rule Pandoraes thoughts,
> And fill her with Ambition and Disdaine;
> I will inforse my influence to the worst,
> Least other Planets blame my regiment.
>
> (II.i.2–5)

And immediately Pandora remarks:

> Though rancor now be rooted from my hart,
> I feel it burdened in an other sort:
> By day I think of nothing but of rule,
> By night my dreames are all of Empery.
> Mine eares delight to heare of Soveraigntie,
> My tongue desires to speak of princly sway,
> My eye would every object were a crowne.
>
> (II.i.6–12)

Thereupon Pandora becomes haughty, insolent, and "filled with proud disdain."[13] She demands exaggerated demonstrations of respect from the shepherds, making them "kneele and crowche," watch her "stately looks," and "yield applause to every word" she speaks.[14] In the manner of a haughty potentate she commands them forth to slay a "savage Boare" and perform other exploits to please "Her Majestie."

Jupiter must indeed "inforse" his influence "to the worst," for all astrologers generally assign to Jupiter more benevolent influences than these. Although John Indagine reports Jupiter as "the aucthor of rule," he also reports him as the author of "Beauty, richesse, honor, . . . wysedome, knowledge, eloquence, and magnanimitie."[15] And others affirm Jupiter to be "friend and preserver of the life of man," exponent

---

[12] *The Iatromathematica of Hermes Trismegistus,* trans. John Harvey (London, 1583), pp. 9–10.
[13] II.i.73–78.   [14] II.i.84 ff.
[15] *Briefe Introductions in . . . Natural Astrologie, with the nature of the Planets.* Trans. William Warde (London, 1575), sig. Piv.

of "Peace, Love, and Concord," of courage, justice, affability, sobriety.[16]
Perhaps the most explicit authority is Albohazen Haly, who says:

Jupiter . . . makes one . . . honorable, virtuous and pure, of fine reputation, just, morally upright and religious, frank and free, gentle of disposition, quiet, unruffled, eschewing vain things; beloved by people who
perform beautiful and honest deeds, . . . Jupiter teaches and fosters goodness, shrinks from evil, assists the poor, and governs whatever is commodious or agreeable. He is truthful in speech, honest in deed, and fortunate in
all his activities and influences, loving councils of wise men, just ordinances,
and discriminating judgments.[17]

But if unfortunately situated, Jupiter could be somewhat malicious.
For Ptolemy writes:

Jupiter . . . posited ingloriously . . . will endow the mind with . . . pro-
fusion, . . . bigotry, . . . arrogance, . . . folly, . . . carelessness, and in-
difference.[18]

Augier Ferrier points out that Jupiter likewise situated

will give sometimes foolishness, . . . pryde, . . . prodigalitie; . . . yeeld
hym an hypocrite, . . . and in place of honestie, it will make hym dreame
of tyranny.[19]

Thus Lyly is justified in maintaining that even the benefic Jupiter's
influence could be detrimental, causing one to become haughty, overly
ambitious, and commanding.

When Mars assumes control over Pandora, he says:

> Now bloody Mars begins to play his part,
> Ile worke such warre within Pandoraes breast,
> That after all her churlishness and pride
> She shall become a vixen Martialist.
> (II.i.177–180)

[16] Claudius Dariot, *A Briefe and Most Easie Introduction to the Astrologicall
Judgement of the Starres.* Trans. Fabian Withers (London, 1598), sig. Div; Erra
Pater, *The Book of Knowledge: treating of the Wisdom of the Ancients.* Trans.
William Lilly (New York, 1794), p. 41. Cf. also *The Beginning of Wisdom, An
Astrological Treatise by Abraham ibn Ezra,* trans. and edited by Raphael Levy
and Francisco Cantara (Baltimore, 1939), pp. 195–196.

[17] *Libri de judiciis astrorum* (Basle, 1551), pp. 169, 10. Cf. also Claudius Ptolemy, *op. cit.,* Bk. II, ch. ix and Bk. IV, ch. x (Ashmand ed., pp. 59, 139); Guido
Bonatus, *op. cit.,* col. 101; Bartholomaeus Anglicus, *op. cit.,* Bk. VIII, ch. 22 (Batman ed., London, 1582).

[18] *Op. cit.,* Bk. IV, ch. xviii (Ashmand ed., p. 111).

[19] *Op. cit.,* pp. 13–14. Notice Pandora's "dreames . . . of Empery" and her
"pride" (mentioned below by Mars).

His influence is so devastating that not only Pandora is affected but also the shepherds, who fall into dispute over the boar they have killed. Pandora snatches a spear and puts them all to rout, screaming at them as they flee, "Fyre of debate is kindled in my hart." [20] Then Mars remarks:

> Mars hath inforst Pandora 'gainst her kinde,
> To manage armes and quarrel with her friends:
> And thus I leave her, all incenst with yre:
> Let Sol cool that which I have set on fire.
> (11.i.236-239)

That the bloody, ireful, and otherwise malefic planet Mars conduces to war, fire, strife, debate, and quarreling is attested by all of the astrologers. Albohazen Haly describes the general nature of Mars thus:

Mars is a planet . . . fiery and violent; he is a destroyer and a conqueror, delighting in slaughter and death, in quarrels, brawls, disputes, contests, and other contraventions; he is . . . quickly moved to vehement and devastating anger, . . . He is instrumental in stirring up seditions; he inspires wars and battles and rules over the ravaging and laying waste of lands, over pillage, plundering, ruin, and destruction.[21]

Ptolemy writes:

Mars . . . makes men . . . warlike, . . . daring, bold, . . . contemptuous, tyrannical; . . . cruel, sanguinary, . . . boisterous, ruffian-like, . . . rapacious, pitiless, . . . hostile.[22]

Abraham ibn Ezra concurs:

Mars . . . prognosticates flames of fire, rebellion, . . . disputes, blows, . . . combat, wrath, insults, . . . effrontery, . . . assault, . . . cruelty, . . . brewers of quarrels, . . . destruction and ruin.[23]

Inasmuch as the astrologers have thus considered the war-star Mars second only to Saturn as a powerful begetter of evil, tempestuousness, and mishap, Lyly has therefore employed the influences of Mars correctly.

When Sol assumes control of Pandora's affairs, he remarks:

---

[20] 11.i.220.

[21] *Op. cit.*, (Basle, 1531), p. 11; cited by W. C. Curry, *Chaucer and the Mediaeval Sciences* (New York, 1926), p. 123.

[22] *Op. cit.*, Bk. iii, ch. xviii (Ashmand ed., p. 112). Cf. also Lilly, *op. cit.*, pp 40-42.

[23] *Op. cit.*, Levy and Cantara ed., pp. 197-198.

> But as myselfe by nature am inclinde,
> So shall she now become, gentle and kinde,
> Abandoning all rancor, pride, and rage,
> And changing from a Lion to a Lambe;
> She shall be loving, liberall, and chaste,
> Discreete and patient, mercifull and milde,
> Inspired with poetry and prophesie,
> And vertues apperteyning womanhoode.
>
> (III.i.3–10)

Lyly, we notice, is precisely correct in having Pandora abandon rancor (from Saturn), pride (from Jupiter), and rage (from Mars). As the only planet to shed benevolent influences on Pandora, Sol makes her sweet-tempered and poetical. She apologizes for her preceding hostility, selects Stesias for her husband, and prophesies their marital happiness in oracular verse.[24] Ferrier says that Sol makes one

mannerly, wise, prudent, a lover of nobleness, following glory and honour, gyven to justice, . . . worthy, and of great estimation.[25]

Firmicus Maternus reports that Sol makes one

completely trustworthy, . . . proud but wise, and governs all with moderation and humanity; . . . husbandry, efficiency, judiciousness.[26]

Alchabitius says:

Sol signifies friendliness, . . . mildness, and all virtues generating from honesty. He signifies oratory, mature counsel, stern judgment, magnificence.[27]

Albohazen Haly adds:

Sol . . . makes men of dignity and high principles; he creates extraordinary discourse; an exalted, honest, liberal, and glorious soul who rejoices in sumptuous apparel but is not given to gluttony.[28]

When Venus ascends, she says:

> Phoebus away, . . .
> Ile have her wittie, quick, and amorous,
> Delight in revels and in banqueting,
> Wanton discourses, musicke, and merrie songes.
>
> . . . . . . . . . . . . . .

[24] III.i.11 ff.    [25] *Op. cit.,* p. 14v.
[26] Cited in Johannes Baptista Porta, *Physiognomiae Coelestis Libri Sex* (Rothomagi, 1650), p. 42.
[27] *Loc. cit.*    [28] *Loc. cit.*

> And being so fayre my beames shall make her light,
> For Levety is Beauties wayting mayde.
> Away with chastity and modest thoughts,
>
> . . . . . . . . . . . . .
>
> Set me Pandora in a dauncing vayne.
>
> (III.ii.1-29)

In consequence, Pandora dances and sings and invites all the shepherds to a banquet. Her brain is filled with "hony thoughts." She is so in love with love (she says) that she will be "as loose as Helen" and make her husband twenty-times a cuckold. After making love in turn to each of the shepherds, she intrigues even with the clown Gunophilus.[29]

Some of these qualities and actions are those generally bestowed upon one by Venus if she is fortunately posited in the heavens, undisturbed by unfortunate aspects from the evil planets. Ferrier records:

Venus . . . in good disposition, maketh the man pleasant, merry, dauncing, laughing, content, amiable, gracious, and of good conversation.[30]

Indagine says:

Venus, being temperate, causeth a man to be a lover of . . . playes, songes and bankettes, and all things perteyning to mirth.[31]

Albohali says:

Venus . . . in a favorable position, makes one love to dance and sing; . . . delight in intrigues, fine forms, and good manners.[32]

Firmicus Maternus writes:

Venus makes a person . . . joyous and cheerful, . . . passionate and voluptuous by nature but religious and righteous, . . . rejoice in the practice of music and the arts, . . . achieve many amatory affairs.[33]

Albohazen Haly affirms:

Venus makes singers and charming people, ardent lovers of flowers and elegance. . . . They have genteel manners, . . . are given to games and various diversions, to laughter and joyous living, rejoicing in the companionship of friends and in eating and drinking. They are benevolent, tender by nature, soft and gentle-voiced.[34]

Pandora's unlady-like characteristics and unseemly behavior, however, are bestowed by Venus when she is unfavorably posited. This benevo-

---

[29] III.ii.37 ff.    [30] *Op. cit.,* p. 14.    [31] *Op. cit.,* sig. L2v.
[32] Cited by Porta, *op. cit.,* pp. 47-48.    [33] *Loc. cit.*    [34] *Loc. cit.*

lent planet has a darker side when she is malignantly situated, about which qualities and influences the authorities have not left us in doubt. Says Ferrier of Venus when she influences unfortunately:

If Venus is unfortunate, it maketh the man . . . too merry, . . . given to voluptuousness.[35]

William Lilly reports:

When Venus is ill-dignified, [she causes one to be] . . . riotous, wholly given to dissipation, . . . coveting unlawful beds, incestuous, adulterous, spending his means in ale-houses, taverns, among scandalous and loose people.[36]

Albohazen Haly writes that Venus unfortunately aspected by Mars produces a person

of passionate disposition, . . . a reveler, a dishonorer, a teller of lies, a deceiver of friends and others, . . . successful in satisfying his desires, . . . a scoffer, a reprobate, busily engaged in conceiving corrupt acts and in the practice of abominable fornication.[37]

And such a person Pandora apparently becomes.

The planet Mercury then asserts himself thus:

> Now is Pandora in my regiment,
> And I will make her false and full of slights,
> Theevish, lying, suttle, eloquent;
> For these alone belong to Mercury.
>                                  (iv.i.8–11)

Shortly thereafter the shepherds inform Stesias that Pandora has been unfaithful and lascivious; but Pandora, "Fenced with her tongue, and guarded with her wit," persuades Stesias that the swains have jealously created a device to undo her. She comments to herself:

> My wit is plyant and invention sharpe,
> To make these novices that injure me.
>                                  (iv.i.131–132)

Ingenuously she persuades the shepherds to tell Stesias that their slanders were deceits. Then she steals her husband's pearls and other jewels and elopes with Gunophilus.[38]

Lyly follows the astrologers in having Mercury make one false, thievish, lying, subtle, witty, inventive, and eloquent. Indagine says:

[35] *Op. cit.,* p. 14.     [36] *Op. cit.,* pp. 45–46.
[37] Cited by Porta, *op. cit.,* p. 77.     [38] iv.i.260 ff.

Mercury is the minister and gever of wisdome and eloquence, . . . rheto-
ricke, subtile workes, . . . and such like.[39]

Ferrier writes:

Mercury . . . makes one . . . full of wit; . . . a poet, an Orator, . . .
If evilly disposed, it makes him . . . inconstant, a lyer, a mocker, a deceiver.[40]

Erra Pater remarks that Mercury makes one

eloquent in his Speech, and yet addicted to lying; and if he be poor, he is
commonly light fingered.[41]

Ptolemy writes that Mercury promotes

thievish propensities, robberies, and plots of treachery; . . . renders the
mind clever, . . . inventive, . . . skilful in argument; . . . but [also]
. . . void of truth, . . . inconstant, avaricious, unjust, . . . of slippery
intellect.[42]

And William Lilly says Mercury is

the author of subtlety, tricks, devices, perjury, &c., [and makes one] A
troublesome wit, . . . a great liar; . . . false, . . . cheating and thieving
everywhere.[43]

While Pandora and Gunophilus are in flight, the Moon assumes
control and says:

> Now other planets influence is done,
> To Cynthia, lowest of the erring starres,
> Is beauteous Pandora given in charge.
> And as I am, so shall Pandora be,
> New Fangled, fyckle, slothfull, foolish, mad.
> (v.i.1–6)

Whereupon Pandora becomes "faynt and weary," and vacillates in her
purpose of fleeing further. For this attitude Gunophilus perceives that
she has become "Lunaticke." [44] Stesias overtakes them; and when he
prepares to kill Pandora for her unfaithfulness and treachery, the
planets and Nature intercede and dissuade him from this action.[45] Nature allows Pandora to choose one of the seven planetary spheres in
which to make her abode.[46] In choosing the sphere of the Moon, Pandora says:

[39] *Op. cit.,* sig. L2v.      [40] *Op. cit.,* p. 14.      [41] *Op. cit.,* p. 42.
[42] *Op. cit.,* Bk. ii, ch. ix (Ashmand ed., p. 60), and Bk. iii, ch. xviii, p. 113.
[43] *Op. cit.,* pp. 48–49.      [44] v.i.7–66.      [45] v.i.251 ff.      [46] v.i.267 ff.

> Cynthia made me idle, mutable,
> Forgetful, foolish, fickle, franticke, madde;
> These be the humours that content me best,
> And therefore will I stay with Cynthia.
>                                           (v.i.307–310)

Stesias is assigned to attend Pandora as the Man in the Moon, Gunophilus the Clown is changed into the familiar hawthorn bush, and
the play ends.

Lyly is in agreement with the astrologers in describing the qualities
and influences of the Moon. Indagine says:

The Moon doth brede instability, . . . causeth madness, unstedfastness,
. . . and sloth.[47]

Ferrier comments that the Moon gives one "inconstancie, lightnes of
spirite," [48] and Ptolemy says that Luna makes one "susceptible of
change, . . . obtuse, variable of purpose." [49] Abraham ibn Ezra says
the "human traits" which Luna bestows are "excessive introspection,
meditation in a mind lacking knowledge; amnesia, phobia, indiffer-
ence." [50] And William Lilly writes that Luna makes one "inclined to
flit and shift his habitation; unstedfast, . . . a vagabond, idle person,
. . . delighting to live beggarly and carelessly." [51]

In this manner has Lyly drawn accurately upon the astrology of his
day to motivate his comedy *The Woman in the Moone*. With one
minor exception,[52] the qualities which Lyly assigned rather carefully
and painstakingly to each of the seven planets, and the effects which
they produce on Pandora, are in general those which would have been
admitted by a competent astrologer. His descriptions of planetary
qualities and influences are fundamentally astrological, and are not
supplemented—as are Robert Henryson's in his *Testament of Cresseid*
—by details from such sources as Graeco-Roman mythology and the
dream-allegories.[53] Lyly had probably done some reading on the sub-

---

[47] *Op. cit.,* sigs. P3r, L2v.      [48] *Op. cit.,* p. 14.
[49] *Op. cit.,* Bk. III, ch. xviii, p. 113.
[50] *Op. cit.,* p. 202.      [51] *Op. cit.,* p. 51.
[52] That is, the "passions of the heart" which Lyly assigns to Saturn are stated
by Hermes Trismegistus to be under the jurisdiction of Mars and Sol.
[53] Cf. Marshall W. Stearns, "The Planet Portraits of Robert Henryson," *PMLA,*
LIX (1944), 911–927.

ject,[54] but he was certainly more vitally concerned in making astrology embellish his play than in making his play expound astrology. Lyly was not interested chiefly in astrology; he was interested in producing a dramatic comedy. But his audience—the courtly circle—had by this time become at least cognizant of and probably fascinated by Dr. John Dee's horoscope-casting for London aristocrats. It is quite reasonable to suppose that Lyly, with an eye out for any trick that might advance his fortunes and at the same time give his play virtuosity and novelty, motivated his comedy with astral influences to make it particularly attractive to astrology-minded spectators at Whitehall. In any case, Lyly's idea of motivating an entire play by means of planetary influences was original, novel, and—I have no doubt—highly amusing to his audience.[55]

[54] Obviously I do not maintain that any of the sources I have cited were specifically used by Lyly.

[55] Bond maintains that *The Woman in the Moone* "is probably indebted to the example of Greene's *Planetomachia*, published in 1585; and to the dramatic example of *The Rare Triumphs of Love and Fortune*, published in 1589." This is one means he employs to date the composition of Lyly's play as of 1591. See Bond, *op. cit.*, III, 324. I can find very little, if any, internal evidence that Lyly's play is indebted to either Greene's *Planetomachia* or the anonymous *Rare Triumphs of Love and Fortune*.

## CHAPTER FIVE

# ATEUKIN THE ASTROLOGER IN
# ROBERT GREENE'S *James the Fourth*

IT HAS BEEN KNOWN a long time that the plot of Robert Greene's
*Scottish Historie of James the Fourth,* a "history play" which glaringly
departs from the facts and conditions of the actual Scottish king's
reign, is based not on historical facts but on the first *novella* of the
third decade of Giraldi Cinthio's *Hecatommithi.*[1] Although the Italian
source and Greene's distortion of history may be granted, it has been
shown recently that the character Ateukin—a person not found in
Cinthio's story—was modeled upon an actual charletan named John
Damian, who not only duped James IV with all sorts of fraudulent ex-
periments but was also well known in historical tradition for doing
so. From Holinshed and other contemporary chroniclers we learn that
the unscrupulous Damian ingratiated himself with the Scottish king
by his pretense of skill in mysterious and secret matters and then con-
tinued to abuse the king's confidence by practicing alchemy and other
frauds. That Greene was probably acquainted with the historical tradition concerning this parasitic sharper and modeled Ateukin somewhat
upon him has been convincingly shown by Professor Waldo F. Mc-
Neir,[2] although McNeir has not properly delineated the fact that in
historical tradition Damian was chiefly an alchemist whereas in
Greene's play he is chiefly an astrologer. At any rate, no one has ex-
amined the astrological manifestations with which Ateukin crawls
into King James' favor. I find that such an examination yields interesting results, and shows that Ateukin's analysis of the king's horoscope has considerable technical significance.

---

[1] J. Churton Collins, ed., *The Plays and Poems of Robert Greene* (Oxford,
1905), II, 79 ff.
[2] "The Original of Ateukin in Greene's *James IV,*" *MLN,* LXII (1947), 376–
381.

Although recently married to Dorothea, the daughter of the English sovereign, King James of Scotland in Greene's play is smitten by the beauty of a lady of the court named Ida. While James one day ponders aloud the dilemma which his amorous fancy has got him into, Ateukin, a penniless foreign adventurer, is lurking about to discover some means of getting himself into the king's favor. When Ateukin overhears this secret and solitary confession of James, he immediately steps forward and introduces himself to the king as

> a man of Art,
> Who knowes, by constellation of the stars,
> By opposition and by drie [dire] aspects,
> The things are past and those that are to come.
>
> (II.301–304) [3]

Even when the king boxes Ateukin on the ear for his impertinent and saucy intrusion, Ateukin continues:

> 'Tis inconvenient, Mighty Potentate, . . .
> To scorne the sooth of science with contempt.
> I see in those imperiall lookes of yours
> The whole discourse of love: Saturn combust
> With direful lookes, at your nativitie
> Beheld faire Venus in her silver orbe;
> I know, by certain axioms I have read,
> Your graces griefs, and further can expresse
> Her name that holds you thus in fancies bands.
>
> . . . . . . . . . . . . . . . .
>
> 'Tis Ida is the mistresse of your heart.
>
> (II.315–327)

Amazed that the man can know his secret, the credulous James becomes quickly convinced of Ateukin's "Art," and, when Ateukin thereupon promises to dissolve him from his marriage and secure Ida for him, James promises to "exalt" the villain above all others in his kingdom. [4]

Ateukin has informed us, of course, very little about the king's nativity: he has not told us the sign in the ascendant, nor the houses or

---

[3] I cite throughout from the edition of Collins, *op. cit.*

[4] James shows immediately that he knows little of astrology; otherwise he would observe that the science provides no means whereby Ateukin could actually discover the *name* of "Her . . . that holds you thus in fancies bands."

signs in which the planets are placed—all of which is vitally necessary
for the complete interpretation of a horoscope. We know only that

> Saturn combust,
> With direful lookes, at your nativitie
> Beheld faire Venus in her silver orbe.

But Saturn's being "combust" means that Saturn was within 8½ degrees of the Sun, or, in short, that Saturn and Sol were in platic conjunction.[5] That Saturn "beheld" Venus means that these two planets
were aspecting one another;[6] and since the aspect was "direful" we
may take it to be either *quadrat* or *opposition*—the two malefic aspects
in astrology.[7] And furthermore, if Saturn in conjunction with Sol was
in quadrat aspect with Venus, it follows by simple analysis that Sol
and Venus were also in quadrat aspect.

Ateukin leads the king to believe that this configuration reveals
"The whole discourse of love" and presages for him a union with
Ida. But according to Claudius Dariot, whose popular astrological
textbook was published frequently throughout the latter part of the
sixteenth century, it really presages nothing of the sort. In a chapter
entitled "How to know whether a man shall obtaine that woman in
marriage which he desireth," Dariot observes:

> This question being proposed, . . . If the lord of the ascendant or the
> *Moone* bee in the seventh house, and the *Sunne* do behold or apply unto
> *Venus,* it signifieth that the marriage shall come to passe, but with much
> labour and difficultie, and especially if the aspects be of enmitie, for these
> aspects breede hatred and displeasure, and destroy the worke, except some
> other better significations come between. But if the lord of the seventh
> house bee placed in the first, . . . or that *Venus* doth behold by a trine

---

[5] Cf. William Lilly, *Christian Astrology* (London, 1647, 1939), p. 339; "*Combustion:* The being within 8°30' of the Sun, which is said to burn up those planets
near him, so that they lose their power. It is always evil testimony."

[6] Strictly speaking, a planet or sign "beholds" another only when each planet
or sign is equidistant from either of the two tropical signs, Cancer and Capricorn.
Cf. Claudius Ptolemy, *Quadripartitum,* trans. J. M. Ashmand (London, 1822;
Chicago, 1936), Bk. i, ch. xviii; and Claudius Dariot, *A Briefe and most easie
Introduction to the Astrological Judgement of the Starres,* trans. Fabian Withers
(London, 1598), ch. vii.

[7] The *quadrat* (modern equivalent: *quartile,* or *square*) aspect means the
planets so aspected are posited in the circle of the heavens 90 degrees apart; *opposition* means they are a half-circle, or 180 degrees, apart. Cf. figure, p. 105.

or sextile aspect the *Sunne,* the querent shall easily obtaine his wife. If this be one by quadrat or opposition, it shall hardly come to passe.[8]

Thus the aspect between Sol and Venus is vitally concerned with determining a man's prospective marriage partner. But Ateukin persuades James to believe that the configuration means precisely the opposite of what it does mean: for the quadrat aspect between Sol and Venus means that James shall not possess Ida. And, in fact, he never does, either in matrimony or otherwise.

It is interesting to note, however, that these particular configurations of Saturn, Sol, and Venus in the king's nativity would, according to the astrologers, endow James with precisely such qualities as he exhibits throughout the play, and would presage for him such fortunes— or misfortunes—as he encounters. According to William Lilly, most renowned of England's seventeenth-century astrologers, Saturn conjunct with Sol signifies

losses . . . by men in power, who persecute the native for some contempt of the law. . . . The native is generally very disagreeable, deceitful, mistrustful, and unfortunate; always losing his property by speculation, which in the end often brings him to ruin; particularly if the native have anything to do with the government, or with the state.[9]

Zadkiel, a nineteenth-century astrologer (who based his judgments upon the Mediaeval and Renaissance astrological writers), agrees that a conjunction of Sol and Saturn presages

Destruction to the native's fame and credit, loss of good name, &c. He is robbed and cheated by servants, tenants, &c., and is full of heavy thoughts, and suffers much vexation, . . . To a king, defeat, &c.[10]

Another configuration of the king's horoscope, Saturn in quadrat to Venus, denotes

losse of goods, . . . uncivility; . . . hys wives shall love him effectually, although they dissemble theyr love; . . . it maketh him evill disposed, . . . lecherous, infamous by reason of woman.[11]

And Claudius Ptolemy says that this configuration

---

[8] *Op. cit.,* sigs. P2r–P3v.      [9] *Op. cit.,* p. 317.

[10] Zadkiel [J. M. Morrison], *The Grammar of Astrology* (London, 1852; appended to Lilly, *op. cit.,* London, 1939), p. 481. Cf. also Firmicus Maternus, *Matheseos Libri VIII,* ed. W. Kroll and F. Skutsch (Lipsiae, 1897), pp. 116–117.

[11] Augier Ferrier, *A Learned Astronomical Discourse of the Judgement of Nativities,* trans. Thomas Kelway (London, 1593), pp. 39v–40v.

makes men licentious and libidinous, practisers of lewdness, careless, . . . treacherous to women, especially to those of his own family; wanton, quarrelsome, sordid; slanderous, superstitious, adulterous, and impious; blasphemers of the gods, and scoffers at holy rites.[12]

The quadrat aspect between Sol and Venus (says Zadkiel) influences a person

to impure conduct and sordid actions. He incurs discredit and scandal. He has differences with females, is refused marriage, quarrels with his wife, &c.[13]

And Ferrier remarks:

The quadrat of the Sunne and Venus signifieth . . . lust, deceite by women, inconstancie, . . .[14]

Now an examination of the characteristics and misfortunes of the king as exhibited throughout the play shows that these configurations in his nativity bring upon him all these tidings which would be prognosticated by the astrologers. In fact, the entire play evolves around James' deceit and lustfulness, his "differences" with women, his undoing by those at court and by Ateukin, his double-dealings which bring him virtually to the brink of ruin.

James' unseemly love for Ida and his disregard for his wife Dorothea is soon discovered by all the people at court. Sir Bertram disgustingly observes that "our king . . . makes love" to Ida by extravagant gifts.[15] Douglas speaks of James' "deceitful" love for Ida, his "careless estimate" of Dorothea, and says of James' disagreeable nature:

> If we but enter presence of his grace
> Our payment is a frowne, a scoffe, a frumpe.[16]

The Bishop of St. Andrews remarks:

> Seeing his highnesse reachlesse course of youth,
> His lawlesse and unbridled vaine of love,
> His too intentive trust to flatterers,
> His abject care of councell of his friendes,

---

[12] *Op. cit.*, Bk. iii, ch. xviii. Incidentally, Don Cameron Allen, "Science and Invention in Greene's Prose," *PMLA*, liii (1938), 1007–1018, strongly suggests Greene's use of Ptolemy's *Quadripartitum* in Greene's *Planetomachia;* but see Johnstone Parr, "Sources of the Astrological Prefaces in Greene's *Planetomachia,*" *SP*, xlvi (1949), 400–410.

[13] *Op. cit.*, p. 438.     [14] *Op. cit.*, pp. 39r–40v.
[15] Lines 585–586.     [16] Lines 965, 957–958.

> Cannot but greeve; . . .
> I, for my part,—(let others as they list!)—
> Will leave the Court.[17]

Ateukin finally suggests that James consent to the murder of Dorothea, and James, unable to secure Ida any other way, gives his approval. Learning of the king's plans to have her killed, Lord Ross advises Dorothea to flee the court in disguise. After the queen has (supposedly) been murdered and James is thus assured of Ida's submission to him, James learns that Ida has meanwhile wed Lord Eustace. Whereupon the jilted king exclaims:

> How have the partial heavens, then, dealt with me!
> Boading my weale, for to abase my power!
> Alas what thronging thoughts do me oppresse!
> Injurious love is partial in my right,
> And flattering tongues, by whom I was misled,
> Have laid a snare to spoyle my state & me.[18]

Thus James perceives that not only the stars but also his servants have deceived him, and at last realizes that he has been guilty of great sin. But he repents too late, for Andrew has informed the English king of Dorothea's murder, and war is initiated between England and Scotland. Just as the English king demands surrender, Dorothea appears, healed of her wounds which were thought by her murderer to be fatal. Dorothea forgives James for his sins, the two kings are reconciled, and the play ends.

Until this "surprise ending," James may be said to be the living embodiment of a man whose horoscope contained malignant aspects between Saturn, Venus, and the Sun. He is tricked by a man whom he has placed "in power," and is persecuted "for contempt of the law"; he is disagreeable, deceitful, mistrustful, and unfortunate; he almost loses his kingdom in the war—all of which William Lilly would have predicted. His fame, credit, and good name have been tossed to the winds because of his unlawful love for Ida, and he is cheated by his servant—as Ferrier and Zadkiel would have presaged. He is dissipated, lewd, and careless of his office; he is "treacherous to women, especially to those of his own family"; he is wanton, quarrelsome, superstitious, impious—all of which Ptolemy would have said. His inconstancy in-

---

[17] Lines 927–935.     [18] Lines 2236–2249.

curs "discredit and scandal" and "differences with females"; he is "refused marriage" and "quarrels with his wife"—as Ferrier and Zadkiel would prognosticate. All of this strongly suggests that Greene's selection of these astral configurations which form a part of the king's horoscope was not haphazard and aimless.

We might even suppose that Greene's Elizabethan audience, probably familiar with such configurations, recognized to some extent the significance of Ateukin's astrological allusion. The Elizabethan world was in many respects quite different from our own, and consequently the motives for action and character used by a sixteenth-century dramatist are frequently quite different from those employed by a modern playwright. We have forgotten Fortune's wheel, the four humours, the stars; the Elizabethan decidedly had not, and he utilized often these springs of human action and character which a modern dramatist never thinks of. To most Elizabethans astrological motivation was not a mere figurative embellishment. We moderns are prone to overlook the probable fact that Shakespeare, for example, actually meant for the stars to "cross" the destinies of Romeo and Juliet quite as much as the chance delay of good Friar John's letter—simply because we are unfamiliar with Renaissance concepts and with the mind of the Elizabethan audience for whom the play was first written.

*CHAPTER SIX*

# SHAKESPEARE'S ARTISTIC USE
# OF ASTROLOGY

ALTHOUGH SHAKESPEARE'S collected plays include more than a hundred separate astrological allusions, the ideas found in the majority of such references are little more than mere commonplaces. In his use of astrology we have another illustration of how a master artist works, of how the true creative genius may be master of no field of knowledge and yet possess a sixth sense and a sponge-like capacity for absorbing essentials of knowledge in any field. Although his plays as a whole teem with allusions to the influence of the stars, it is not apparent that Shakespeare knew the technicalities of astrology any more than did his fellow dramatists—indeed, if as much.

But that human beings are but helpless puppets of the stars is stated definitely and continuously from *Titus Andronicus* to *The Winter's Tale*. The dukes of Bedford and Exeter affirm that the stars "consented unto Henry's death" and "plotted" his "overthrow."[1] The dauphin Charles comments that Mars' shining upon the French caused them to be victorious in battle against the English.[2] The "star-cross'd" Romeo believes the apothecary's poison is the only thing that will "shake the yoke of inauspicious stars" from his "world-wearied flesh."[3] Antony attributes his first defeat to the fact that the stars have forsaken him; the moon's eclipse, he says, portends his ultimate fall; and Octavius Caesar laments that his stars and those of Antony made the two generals "unreconcilable."[4] Pericles attributes the loss of all his fortunes to the "ire" of "angry stars."[5] Prospero's powers and fortunes, he says, depend upon "a most auspicious star."[6] Hermione attributes her unjust

---

[1] *I King Henry VI*, I.i.5, 23.    [2] *Ibid.*, I.ii.1–4.
[3] *Romeo and Juliet*, Prologue 6; v.iii.109–112.
[4] *Antony and Cleopatra*, III.xiii.143–47; III.xxx.154–56; v.i.46–48.
[5] *Pericles*, II.i.1–9.    [6] *The Tempest*, I.ii.180–84.

treatment and imprisonment to the fact that "some ill planet reigns." [7]
Others throughout the plays advocate the same belief. [8]

Often Shakespeare's characters maintain that one's fate and disposition depend upon the stars at one's birth and their relationship with other stars at that time. Julia tells Lucetta that Proteus is not a deceitful lover because "truer stars did govern Proteus' birth." [9] Richard III informs Elizabeth that the princes were murdered because "at their birth good stars were opposite." [10] King Henry VI explains metaphorically that Warwick's horoscope contains "an olive branch and laurel crown." [11] Glendower tells that at his birth the heavens were ominously "full of fiery shapes." [12] And Hermione's third baby was "starred most unluckily." [13]

Throughout Shakespeare's plays we find that a character's immediate actions and undertakings might be favored or hindered by the stars: planets might strike felling blows at man, be responsible for various disasters (especially plagues), and bode much ill-fortune if they wandered from their "spheres." These are the tenets of astrology, incidentally, that Shakespeare used most. A "happy star" leads the Goths to Rome as captives and then exalts them in fortune. [14] It is "a lowering star" that seeks "subversion" of the harmless life of Humphrey. [15] "Some consequence yet hanging in the stars" begins his date with the night's eventful revels at the Capulet home. [16] Orsino is certain that Viola's "constellation is right apt" for her mission to Olivia; and Sebastian's "stars shine darkly" over him. [17] Helena's legacy of her father's prescription is "sanctified by the luckiest stars in heaven." [18] Iago says that the participants of the street-brawl acted "as if some planet had unwitted" them; and Othello assigns the dreadful deeds at the end of the

---

[7] *The Winter's Tale*, II.i.105–107.

[8] See *I King Henry VI*, IV.v.6; *II King Henry VI*, V.ii.73; *III King Henry VI*, IV.vi.19–22; *Richard III*, IV.iv.215–217; *Twelfth Night*, I.iv.35; II.i.3–7; *King Lear*, I.i.113–115; I.ii.112–126; *Troilus and Cressida*, I.iii.85–102; *Richard II*, II.iv.7–17; *Measure for Measure*, III.i.6–11; *Julius Caesar*, II.ii.30–31; *Othello*, V.ii.98–101; V.ii.109–111; *Timon of Athens*, IV.iii.1–11; IV.iii.109–110.

[9] *Two Gentlemen of Verona*, II.vii.74–78.

[10] *Richard III*, IV.iv.215.                         [11] *I King Henry VI*, IV.vi.34.

[12] *I King Henry IV*, III.i.11.                      [13] *The Winter's Tale*, III.ii.98–101.

[14] *Titus Andronicus*, IV.ii.32–34.                 [15] *II King Henry VI*, III.i.206–208.

[16] *Romeo and Juliet*, I.iv.106–113.                [17] *Twelfth Night*, I.iv.36–37; II.i.4.

[18] *All's Well*, I.iii.248–252.

play to "the very error of the moon . . . that makes men mad." [19] Talbot blames the "malignant and ill-boding stars" for drawing his young son into the deadly turmoil of the war. [20] Pericles plans to remain in Tarsus "Until our stars that frown lend us a smile," and affirms that his daughter's life is saved because "her better stars brought her to Mytilene." [21] Hermione resolves to be patient in her misfortune until the heavens "look with an aspect more favorable." [22] Marcus hopes that some planet will "strike" him down. [23] Marcellus tells of a time so hallowed that even the planets cannot "strike." [24] Biron says that "stars pour down plagues for perjury." [25] Timon of Athens wishes the invading Alcibiades to be to the Athenians "as a planetary plague." [26] Ulysses remarks that when the planets wander from their places there immediately follow plagues, mutinies, changes, and horrors which "Divert / The unity and married calm of states / Quite from their fixture." [27] Antony's "good stars" that were his "former guides" deserted their "orbs" and "shot their fires into the abysm of hell." [28]

Several of Shakespeare's characters are governed by particular stars, and Shakespeare is always consistent in assigning the planet which would endow the appropriate qualities. Posthumus was born under the benevolent planet Jupiter, and consequently has a favorable destiny at the end of the play. [29] Monsieur Parolles would be born under Mars because he would be known as a soldier. [30] Elizabeth, who weeps throughout *Richard III* is indeed "governed by the *watery* moon." [31]

---

[19] *Othello*, ii.iii.182–184; v.ii.109–111.

[20] *I King Henry VI*, iv.v.6.   [21] *Pericles*, i.iv.108; v.iii.9–10.

[22] *The Winter's Tale*, ii.i.105–107.   [23] *Titus Andronicus*, ii.iv.14.

[24] *Hamlet*, i.i.162. H. B. Wheatley and P. Cunningham, *London Past and Present* (London, 1891), notice that in olden bills of mortality sudden deaths were frequently entered as "Planet strucken," and that the death certificates of thirteen persons in 1632 listed the cause of death as "Planet struck." See H. H. Carter, ed., *Every Man in His Humour by Ben Jonson* (New Haven, 1921), p. 387.

[25] *Love's Labour's Lost*, v.ii.394.   [26] *Timon of Athens*, iv.iii.108–110.

[27] *Troilus and Cressida*, i.iii.85–102.

[28] *Antony and Cleopatra*, iii.xiii.144–147.

[29] *Cymbeline*, v.iv.106.   [30] *All's Well*, i.i.206–220.

[31] *Richard III*, ii.ii.69. The astrologers assigned *weeping*, however, to Saturn rather than to Luna. Possibly the moon's influence on the tides precipitated Shakespeare's remark here. He makes the same error when (in *MND*, ii.ii.44–46)

Conrade, who was born under Saturn,[32] and Aaron, whose desires Saturn governs,[33] are both fitting exponents of that planet's generally malign influence. Edmund was evilly "compounded under the Dragon's Tail" and the malignant stars of Ursa Major.[34] Autolycus, born under Mercury, the planet of rogues, vagabonds, thieves, and liars, is (as Autolycus says) a "snatcher-up of unconsidered trifles" who skips over the laws of morality at his pleasure.[35] John of Gaunt speaks of England (astrologically?) as "this seat of Mars." [36] Cleopatra, in her final moment of stability, refuses to be governed by the "fleeting" and varying moon.[37] Being born "in a merry hour" and under a star that "danced" is exactly suitable for the mirthful and mischievous Beatrice; and Benedick was, as he says, certainly *not* born under a "rhyming planet" if the best he can do is to rhyme "lady" and "baby." [38]

The signs of the zodiac are mentioned in six of Shakespeare's plays. Only in *Twelfth Night*, however, does the reference connote any

---

he allows Titania to say that the Moon, by washing the air, causes rheumatism; for Saturn is the planet which astrologers hold responsible for rheumatic diseases. In *1 Henry IV*, i.ii.15 ff., Falstaff cries: "We that take purses go by the moon and the seven stars, and not by Phoebus . . . ; we be men of good government as the sea is, by our noble and chaste mistress the moon, under whose countenance we steal." Mercury rather than Luna is the ruling planet of thieves (perhaps Shakespeare means merely that Falstaff steals *at night*); yet William Lilly, *Christian Astrology*, London, 1647, 1939, p. 51, records that Luna, ill-dignified, makes "a mere vagabond, idle person, hating labour; a drunkard, a sot, one . . . delighting to live beggarly and carelessly"—a description that fits Falstaff particularly well. The constellation called the Pleiades (the "seven stars") was dominated by Mars and Luna (cf. Claudius Ptolemy, *Quadripartitum*, I, iv, and Robert Fludd, *Utriusque Cosmi Metaphysica*, . . . II, 583), and one born under an ill-dignified Mars was destined to be (according to astrologers) "a lover of thieving" and "a highway thief" (Lilly, p. 40).

[32] *Much Ado*, i.iii.12.      [33] *Titus Andronicus*, ii.iii.31.

[34] *King Lear*, i.ii.140–144.

[35] *The Winter's Tale*, iv.ii.24–28. That Mercury influenced one to *thievery* and *lying* was probably somewhat common knowledge. Cf. Erra Pater's *The Book of Knowledge*, p. 26: "He that is born in the hour of Mercury . . . is . . . addicted to lying; and if he be poor, he is commonly light fingered."

[36] *Richard II*, ii.i.40. All astrologers were agreed that England is ruled by Aries, whose lord is the planet Mars. Cf. Claudius Ptolemy, *Quadripartitum*, Bk. ii, ch. iii: "Britain, Galatia, Germany, and Barsnia have a greater share of familiarity with Aries and Mars." Cf. also Lilly, *op. cit.*, p. 58.

[37] *Antony and Cleopatra*, v.ii.240.

[38] *Much Ado*, ii.i.247–250; v.ii.36–41.

astrological significance, and even there the allusion is a ludicrous one made by the two boisterous knights of Olivia's household.[39]

Several of the astrological passages in Shakespeare's plays are apostrophic. Falconbridge invokes the stars to help him "push destruction and perpetual shame" from the land.[40] When Romeo hears of Juliet's death, he utters immediately a defiant apostrophe to the stars.[41] Enobarbus remorsefully invokes the moon, "the sovereign mistress of true melancholy," to end his "dispised" life.[42] Timon of Athens invokes the sun to wreak chaos upon everybody's fortunes.[43] The Duke of Bedford admonishes comets to "brandish their crystal tresses in the sky" and to chastise the stars that caused the death of his king.[44] And Camillo prays that "a happy star" will reign over him after he has been forced to flee from the court of Leontes.[45]

Shakespeare's characters frequently express the idea that various celestial phenomena forebode disastrous events to come upon a group of people or upon some particularly important personage. The common harbingers of these unfortunate events were comets, meteors, and eclipses. Bedford informs his companions that comets import "changes of times and states."[46] Charles of France sees in the flaming brand or signal torch "a comet of revenge" and "a prophet to the fall of all our foes."[47] Calpurnia reminds Julius Caesar that not only comets but "The heavens themselves blaze forth the death of princes."[48] Often the wonder and amazement that comets cause among the populace is remarked upon.[49] The Welchmen in *Richard II* leave their ranks and disperse when the "meteors fright the fixed stars from heaven," because the Welchmen fully believe that such a phenomenon portends

---

[39] *Twelfth Night*, i.iii.146–149. The two buffoons, Sir Andrew Aguecheek and Sir Toby Belch, know little astrology. Sir Andrew thinks that the sign Taurus rules the sides and heart of the human body, and is corrected by Sir Toby who contends that it rules the legs and thighs. Both knights, as might be expected, are wrong. Taurus governed the neck and throat, and the most ignorant Elizabethan theatre-goer probably knew it. Such humor is wasted on modern audiences.

[40] *King John*, v.vii.74–78.
[41] *Romeo and Juliet*, v.i.24.
[42] *Antony and Cleopatra*, iv.ix.12–15.
[43] *Timon of Athens*, iv.iii.1–11.
[44] *I King Henry VI*, i.i.3–5.
[45] *The Winter's Tale*, i.ii.263.
[46] *I King Henry VI*, i.i.2.
[47] *I King Henry VI*, iii.ii.31–32.
[48] *Julius Caesar*, ii.ii.30–31.

[49] See *The Taming of the Shrew*, iii.ii.85; *Pericles*, v.i.85–87; *I King Henry IV*, iii.ii.46–47; *King John*, v.ii.53.

"the death and fall" of the king.[50] The Papal legate Pandulph contends that any exhalation in the sky will be looked upon as "meteors, prodigies, and signs" portending the downfall of King John.[51] Prince Hal remarks to Bardolph that the meteors and exhalations portend merely "hot livers and cold purses," but Worcester, who deserted King Henry's forces, is likened to an "exhal'd meteor" and looked upon as "a prodigy of fear" and "a portent of broached mischief to the unborn times." [52]

Many of Shakespeare's astrological allusions are metaphorical. Phebe compares the effect of Rosalind's eyes with the effects of the stars.[53] The flattering Poet in *Timon of Athens* compares the rejected Timon to a star whose nobleness gives life and influence.[54] Leontes compares cuckoldom to "a bawdy planet that will strike / Where 'tis predominant." [55] Prince Hal compares Falstaff and Doll Tearsheet to "Saturn and Venus in conjunction"; and Poins compares Bardolph, heated by the kisses of Dame Quickly, to "the fiery Trigon." [56] Falstaff contends that his cudgel will "hang like a meteor" over the cuckold-horns of Ford and thus "predominate" over him.[57] Parolles affirms that the nobles of the court "move under the influence of the most received star" (i.e., under the influence of the leader of fashion).[58] Cymbeline likens his lost sons and daughter to stars which "started from their orbs" and affirms that since they are happily restored they may "reign in them" again.[59] Queen Margaret compares the face on the severed head of her lover Suffolk to a "wandering planet" that has ruled over her.[60] And Elizabeth, weeping over her deceased husband, exclaims that "all of us have cause / To wail the dimming of our shining star." [61]

All of the astrological predictions in Shakespeare's plays are fulfilled. Romeo's premonition that the stars would loose some malevolent influence at Capulet's feast and bring about a "vile forfeit of untimely

[50] *Richard II*, ii.iv.7–17.      [51] *King John*, iii.iv.155–159.
[52] *I King Henry IV*, ii.iv.351–357; v.i.11–12.
[53] *As You Like It*, iv.iii.50–54.      [54] v.i.65–67.
[55] *The Winter's Tale*, i.ii.200–202.
[56] *II King Henry IV*, ii.iv.286–287, 289–291. A "trigon" is a "triplicity," or a group of three particular signs of the zodiac alike in nature and influence. The "fiery Trigon" consists of Aries, Leo, and Sagittarius, all of which signs are of a hot and dry quality. Cf. Lilly, *op. cit.*, p. 345.
[57] *The Merry Wives of Windsor*, ii.ii.290–295.      [58] *All's Well*, ii.i.54–58.
[59] *Cymbeline*, v.v.370–372.      [60] *II King Henry VI*, iv.iv.15–18.
[61] *Richard III*, ii.ii.101–102.

death"[62] is exactly what happens subsequently. Pandulph's sneering prophecy in *King John* is fulfilled: the people do see signs in the heavens prophesying vengeance upon John.[63] Antony's catastrophe follows hard upon the desertion of his "good stars" and the moon's eclipse that boded his fall.[64] The Welshmen, regarded as superstitious because celestial phenomena threw them into utter consternation, were right after all: their king did die, as the signs predicted.[65] Caesar disregarded Calpurnia's warning about the message of the sky and was stabbed to death at the senate-house.[66] Helena's enterprise that was "sanctified by the luckiest stars in heaven" was successful enough to win her a husband.[67] In Suffolk's nativity it was presaged that he should die "by water"; although he was beheaded, the execution was performed by *pirates*.[68] And all of the "effects" of the eclipses listed in *King Lear* by Gloster (and ridiculed by Edmund) actually follow in the play: unnaturalness between child and parent, divisions in state, mutinies in countries, treason and treachery in palaces, malediction against king, banishment of friends, dissipation of cohorts, nuptial breaches, death.[69]

Shakespeare's characters—like Elizabethans in general—were not always fully certain just how far astral influences extended. The general opinion among them seems to have been that the stars are not omnipotent, but that they strongly incline the soul one way or another and that few men can resist their power. That a person could fight the malignancy of the stars is uniquely illustrated by Bedford when he assumes that King Henry's ghost can "combat with adverse planets in the heavens" and "scourge the revolting stars."[70] Helena understands astrology's limitations when she exclaims:

> Our remedies oft in ourselves do lie,
> Which we ascribe to heaven. The fated sky
> Gives us free scope, only doth backward pull
> Our slow designs when we ourselves are dull.[71]

With reservations Warwick would agree, for he says "Few men rightly

[62] *Romeo and Juliet*, I.iv.106–113.

[63] *King John*, III.iv.155–159; IV.ii.182–189.

[64] *Antony and Cleopatra*, III.xiii.144–147.   [65] *Richard II*, II.iv.7–17.

[66] *Julius Caesar*, II.ii.30–31.   [67] *All's Well*, I.iii.248–252.

[68] *II King Henry VI*, IV.i.34–35; IV.i.   [69] *King Lear*, I.ii.112–165.

[70] *I King Henry VI*, I.i.52–56.

[71] *All's Well*, I.i.231–234. Helena is nevertheless resigned to astral influences three times in the play: I.i.193–198; I.iii.248–252; II.v.79–81.

temper with the stars."[72] Cassius, however, discredits astrology sternly when he reminds Brutus that the blame for being an "underling" lies not in one's stars but in oneself.[73] A condemnation of astrological beliefs is also in Hotspur's mind when he argues rather convincingly with Glendower against the probability of influences of meteors and other celestial phenomena.[74] Cardinal Pandulph's remarks are unquestionably sarcastic when he comments that the common people will call any "natural exhalation in the sky" a meteor, a prodigy, and a sign.[75] And Edmund bluntly characterizes astrology as "the excellent foppery of the world."[76]

Although few of these references indicate any special knowledge, or necessitate here a gloss, we are not quite justified in concluding that Shakespeare possessed only a meagre knowledge of astrology. It is true that he cast no horoscopes for any of his characters as did Chaucer for Constance and the Wife of Bath, and his passages give no indication that he was familiar with the *hyleg,* the *alcocoden,* or the *algebuthar.* But his allusions give evidence enough that he possessed a common or general knowledge of the majority of astrology's tenets—a knowledge of the manner in which the stars were reputed to govern life below. His *dramatis personae* speak of stars, planets, comets, meteors, eclipses, planetary aspects, predominance, conjunction, opposition, retrogradation, and all sorts of astro-meteorology. They know that the Dragon's Tail exerts an evil influence, that Mercury governs lying and thievery, that Luna rules vagabonds and idle fellows, that Saturn is malignant and Jupiter benevolent, that the signs of the zodiac rule the limbs and organs of the body, that planets influence cities and nations, that each trigon or triplicity pertains to one of the four elements, that stars rule immediately as well as at birth, that one with a strong constitution might avert the influence of his stars, and so on. Although they do not go into details regarding the technical workings of the science, his characters on the whole seem to possess a general knowledge of stellar influence on human destiny.

Shakespeare's astrological references are ubiquitous, occurring in his poems, comedies, histories, and tragedies. Sometimes the passages indi-

[72] *III King Henry VI,* iv.vi.28–29.          [73] *Julius Caesar,* i.ii.140–141.
[74] *I King Henry IV,* iii.i.10–50.            [75] *King John,* iii.iv.155–159.
[76] *King Lear,* i.ii.112.

cate that the stars are agents in the plot and action; oftentimes they are mere rhetorical flourishes, embellishments, metaphors. Sometimes they are spoken jestingly by the humorists of the plays; often they are stated quite seriously by the principals. Some of the passages are intended to illustrate character or personal characteristics. A few of them ridicule a belief in astral influence. None connects astrology with medical practice, although it is clear that Shakespeare was aware of the belief that planets and signs of the zodiac influence mental and physical health. No astrologers or almanack-makers appear as characters in his plays.[77] Few allusions are made to the practice of astrologers, the passages almost always referring to the potency of the heavenly bodies themselves. There are just as many astrological references—of various kinds—in the later plays as there are in the early ones.

The use of astrology that looms largest in Shakespeare's dramas is the free utilization of astral philosophy in the creation of some especially artistic and beautiful lines. Innumerable astrological passages in the plays are so composed as to make them particularly striking and dramatically effective. In such lines as the following we see the master artist taking common astral tenets and—apparently not caring whether the resultant astrology is "scientifically" correct or not—remoulding his raw materials into something effective and artistic:

Prospero: I find my zenith doth depend upon
         A most auspicious star, whose influence
         If now I court not, but omit, my fortune
         Will ever after droop.
                      (*The Tempest*, I.ii.181–184)

Richard: Three glorious suns, each one a perfect sun;
        Not separated with the racking clouds,
        But sever'd in a pale, clear-shining sky.
        See, see! they join, embrace, and seem to kiss,
        As if they vow'd some league inviolable:
        Now they are but one lamp, one light, one sun.
        In this the heaven figures some event.
                   (*III King Henry VI*, II.i.26–32) [78]

[77] Shakespeare never uses the words *astrologer* or *astrology*. In *Cymbeline* (III.ii.27) *astrologers* are called "astronomers"; in *Venus and Adonis* (line 509) they are called "star-gazers"; in *Sonnet 107* they are called "augers"; and in *King Lear* (I.ii.142), "sectary astronomical."

[78] Shakespeare almost certainly gets this idea from Pliny's *Natural History* (II.xxxi): "Again, several suns are seen at once, neither above nor below the real

*Falstaff:*   . . . we that take purses go by the moon and the seven
stars, and not by Phoebus, he, that wandring knight so fair.
. . . let me say we be men of good government, being gov-
as the sea is, by our noble and chaste mistress the moon, under whose countenance we steal.

                                                            (*1 King Henry IV*, 1.ii.14–41)

*Romeo:*                                   . . . my mind misgives,
Some consequence yet hanging in the stars
Shall bitterly begin his fearful date
With this night's revels and expire the term
Of a dispised life closed in my breast
By some vile forfeit of untimely death.

                                                            (*Romeo and Juliet*, 1.iv.106–111)

*Othello:*   It is the very error of the moon:
She comes more nearer earth than she was wont,
And makes men mad.

                                                            (*Othello*, v.ii.109–111)

*Ulysses:*   The heavens themselves, the planets, and this centre,
Observe degree, priority, and place,
Insisture, course, proportion, season, form,
Office, and custom, in all line of order:
And therefore is the glorious planet Sol
In noble eminence enthroned and spher'd
Amidst the other; whose medicinable eye
Corrects the ill aspects of planets evil,
And posts, like the commandment of a king,
Sans check to good and bad: but when the planets,
In evil mixture, to disorder wander,
What plagues and what portents! what mutiny!
What raging of the sea! shaking of earth!
Commotion in the winds! frights, changes, horrors,
Divert and crack, rend and deracinate
The unity and married calm of states
Quite from their fixture![79]

                                                            (*Troilus and Cressida*, 1.iii.85–102)

---

sun but at an angle with it, never along side of nor opposite to the earth, and not
at night but either at sunrise or at sunset. . . . In former times three suns have
often been seen at once." Pliny then states the five times when this phenomenon
occurred. See *Pliny's Natural History,* ed. H. Rackham (Loeb Classical Library,
1939), p. 243.

[79] One may notice that it took J. Norden in *Vicissitudo Rerum* (London, 1600)
almost a dozen seven-line stanzas to say virtually the same thing. See D. C. Col-

*Cassius:*    The fault, dear Brutus, is not in our stars,
But in ourselves, that we are underlings.
               (*Julius Caesar,* i.ii.140–141)

*Calpurnia:*    When beggars die, there are no comets seen;
The heavens themselves blaze forth the death of princes.
               (*Julius Caesar,* ii.ii.30–31)

*Richard:*    Lo, at their births good stars were opposite!
               (*Richard III,* iv.iv.212)

*Helena:*    Monsieur Parolles, you were born under a
charitable star.

*Parolles:*    Under Mars, I.

*Helena:*    I especially think under Mars.

*Parolles:*    Why under Mars?

*Helena:*    The wars have kept you so under, that you must
needs be born under Mars.

*Parolles:*    When he was predominant.

*Helena:*    When he was retrograde, I think rather.

*Parolles:*    Why think you so?

*Helena:*    You go so much backward when you fight.

*Parolles:*    I am so full of businesses, I cannot answer
thee acutely.
               (*All's Well,* i.i.206–220)

There are few places in Elizabethan or Jacobean drama where words are used more effectively than in these passages. Although they show a minimum knowledge of astrological technicalities, they doubtless exhibit the most *artistic* use of astrology in the Elizabethan and Jacobean drama.

The purpose in this essay is, of course, to discover Shakespeare's use of astrology—not to ascertain his attitude toward it as a valid or invalid science. Since Shakespeare speaks only through his characters, who oftentimes contradict one another, it is virtually impossible to determine with any certainty what attitude the dramatist entertained. To assume that he believed as did the loyal and good Earl of Kent, the estimable Helena, or the heroic Pericles would be dangerous; to assume that he put his own thought into the mouths of Edmund, Cassius, and the impetuous Hotspur would be equally unwarranted. But inasmuch as in the 400-odd lines of astrological allusion Shakespeare presented

lins' edition of this work, *Shakespeare Association Facsimiles No. 4* (Oxford, 1931).

character after character sanctioning astral influence and allows only
four characters—two villains, the Papal legate, and a "hothead"—to
deride it, it seems hardly likely that he seriously mistrusted the science
himself. At any rate, the numerous astrological passages scattered
throughout his dramatic works indicate that he was at least considerably interested in astrology and that he used the science abundantly in
the creation of some of the most striking passages in his plays.[80]

That Shakespeare incorporated astrology in his plays because it
would have an appeal to the audience there cannot be much doubt.
That he employed it merely for this reason does not explain why there
are many astrological passages in the *Sonnets*. Any theory that Shakespeare used bits of astrological lore as grist for his mill, as trappings for

---

[80] Many articles and monographs on this subject have been written. William
Wilson, *Shakespeare and Astrology* (Boston, 1903), points out some of the obvious examples of Shakespeare's astrological allusions, and suggests that their
consistency throughout his works indicates somewhat more than a passing in-
terest in the subject. Cumberland Clark, *Shakespeare and Science* (Birmingham,
England, 1929), concludes that Shakespeare only as a working dramatist, not as
an individual, adopted and accepted the affirmations of astrology. Carroll Camden, Jr., "Astrology in Shakespeare's Day," *Isis*, xix (1933), 26–73, discusses the
Elizabethan attitude toward astrology and accepts Shakespeare's use of the science
as indicative of its widespread appeal. See also Camden's "Elizabethan Almanacs
and Prognostications," *The Library*, New Series, xii (1931), 84–108, 194–207.
R. H. Darby, "Astrology in Shakespeare's *Lear*," *English Studies*, xx (1938),
250–257, assumes that the references against astrology in *King Lear* were intended to please King James, whose *dicta* against astrologers and other fortune-
tellers were supposedly well-known. D. Fraser-Harris, "Shakespeare and the
Influence of the Stars," *Discovery*, viii (1927), 365–366, and Frederick Schark,
"Shakespeare und die Astrologie," *Hamburger Fremdenblatt*, Seite III (July,
1926), 202a, both conclude that Shakespeare, though well-acquainted with astrological lore, believed not one word of it. Moriz Sondheim, "Shakespeare and the
Astrology of His Time," *Journal of the Warburg Institute*, ii (1938), 243–259,
holds that Shakespeare accepted the doctrine of *astrologia naturalis*, but that he
"did not adhere to the belief in any influence of the stars on the destiny of individuals, of nations, or of rulers," and furthermore "rejected the science of
horoscopy, which claims to foretell the influences emanating from the planets
through studying their position" (p. 258). John W. Draper, "Shakespeare's Star-
Cross'd Lovers," *RES*, xv (1939), 1–19, connects the chief characters in *Romeo
and Juliet* with the four types of humours which are in turn governed by particular planets, suggests that these characters' actions are in accord with the
astrological "hours" of the day, and thus makes the play "an astrological tragedy
of humours." See also E. B. Knobel, "Astronomy and Astrology" in *Shakespeare's
England* (Oxford, 1932), i, 444–461; and Robert Calignoc, "Astrology in Shakespeare," *Occult Review* (London, 1905), pp. 192–196, 220–225, 296–302.

his plays, has definite limitations. Elizabethans possessed a thorough-going belief that the stars and planets, comets and eclipses, exercised at least a limited influence on human beings and mundane affairs; and it was not merely the ignorant who accepted these beliefs. Shakespeare was merely holding an artistically reflecting mirror up to life.

## CHAPTER SEVEN

# THE "LATE ECLIPSES"
## IN *King Lear*

THE LONGEST astrological passage in all Shakespeare's plays is the following from *King Lear* (1.ii.98–141):

*Gloster:*   These late eclipses in the sun and moon portend no good to us; though the wisdom of nature can reason it thus and thus, yet nature finds itself scourged by the sequent effects; love cools, friendship falls off, brothers divide: in cities, mutinies; in countries, discord; in palaces, treason; and the bond crack'd 'twixt son and father. This villain of mine comes under the prediction; there's son against father; the king falls from bias of nature; there's father against child. We have seen the best of our time; machinations, hollowness, treachery and all ruinous disorders follow us disquietly to our graves. Find out this villain, Edmund; it shall lose thee nothing; do it carefully. And the noble and true-hearted Kent banished! his offense, honesty! 'Tis strange.                  (*Exit*)

*Edmund:*   This is the excellent foppery of the world, that, when we are sick in fortune,—often the surfeit of our own behavior,—we make guilty of our disasters the sun, the moon, and stars; as if we were villains on necessity; fools by heavenly compulsion; knaves, thieves, and treachers by spherical predominance; drunkards, liars, and adulterers by an enforc'd obedience of planetary influence; and all that we are evil in, by a divine thrusting on. An admirable evasion of whoremaster man, to lay his goatish disposition to the charge of a star! My father compounded with my mother under the Dragon's Tail, and my nativity was under Ursa Major, so that it follows I am rough and lecherous. Fut! I should have been that I am, had the maidenliest star in the firmament twinckled on my bastardizing. Edgar—

### Enter Edgar

and pat! he comes, like the catastrophe of the old comedy. My cue is villainous melancholy, with a sigh like Tom o' Bedlam. O, these eclipses do portend these divisions! Fa, sol, la, mi.

*Edgar:*   How now, brother Edmund? What serious contemplation are you in?

*Edmund:* I am thinking, brother, of a prediction I read this other day, what should follow these eclipses.

*Edgar:* Do you busy yourself with that?

*Edmund:* I promise you, the effects he writes of succeed unhappily: as of unnaturalness between the child and the parent; death, dearth, dissolutions of ancient amities; divisions in state, menaces and maledictions against king and nobles; needless diffidences, banishment of friends, dissipation of cohorts, nuptial breaches, and I know not what.

*Edgar:* How long have you been a sectary astronomical?

Several critics who believe this passage on the "late eclipses" to be a topical allusion have attempted to turn the celestial universe virtually upside down to discover the actual date of occurrence of the "late eclipses" referred to, and thereby to establish more precisely the date of composition of the play.[1] Almost all these commentators, however, have apparently ignored the fact that in determining the actual phenomena most likely referred to by Shakespeare one should ascertain not only the date and magnitude of the eclipses visible in London but also the published astrological prognostications regarding them—especially since Edmund refers explicitly to "a prediction I *read* this other day . . . and the effects he *writes* of." Unfortunately, almost all of these astrological prognostications—to be distinguished from the common almanacks—are now not extant. There can be little doubt, however, that a series of alarming astrological prognostications—similar to those in 1583 and 1588 [2]—were issued in London between 1600 and 1605 regarding the great conjunction of Saturn and Jupiter in 1603 and the unusual number of solar and lunar eclipses during the period. Yet only one scholar, Dr. G. B. Harrison, has cited a seventeenth-century prognostication which can be juxtaposed with Shakespeare's passage in *King Lear*.[3] I wish to bring to light an apparently hitherto unknown

---

[1] Cf. the numerous articles in the *London Times Literary Supplement* (1933), pp. 856, 878, 909; (1934), p. 12. Cf. also R. H. Darby, "Astrology in Shakespeare's *Lear*," *English Studies*, xx (1938), 250–257; H. H. Furness, *A Variorum Edition of King Lear*, pp. 51–56, 378–381; and Kittredge's widely used edition, in which the allusion is used to determine the date of the play.

[2] Cf. Carroll Camden, Jr., "Elizabethan Almanacs and Prognostications," *The Library*, xii (1931), 84–108, 194–207 (esp. pp. 194–203).

[3] *LTLS* (1933), p. 865. Dr. Harrison cites an almanack-maker's "Epistle" dated "London, February 11, 1605 (–06)" as "one possible source of this passage in *King Lear*."

astrological pamphlet published in London in 1604 which has some
bearing upon this passage in *King Lear*.

In this little booklet by Himbert de Billy entitled *Certaine Wonderful Predictions for seven yeeres ensuing, shewing the Strange and
Wonderful Comets and Meteors, beginning this present yeere 1604,*[4]
Englishmen could have found a somewhat alarming account of the
celestial manifestations of the time. Billy presages for 1605 as follows:

Eclipses (especially of the Sunne) do fall in so fewe yeeres, whereby
greevous and most wretched accidents are presaged. Perhaps these be the
latter days, when as all piety and charity shal waxe colde, truth and justice
shal be oppressed: and all things else shall be mixed, disturbed, and turned
upside down, and the forepart set behinde by torments and seditions: and
finally nothing else shall be expected, but spoyle and ruine of the common
society. . . .

This yeere the Moone shall be twice Eclipsed, and the Sunne once. The
first Eclipse of the Moone . . . on the 23 day of March . . . signifies famine and greevous sicknesses and pestilences, tempestuous and hurtful
windes: . . .

The second Eclipse of the Moone . . . the 17 day of September . . . signifies change of Lawes, Institutions and Sects: and . . . the self-same things
which are mentioned in the yeere 1603 the 14 day of May: . . . [Turning
back to the prognostication for 1603, we find:] . . . the Eclipse of the xiiii
of May . . . proclaymes death unto Kings, Princes, and Ecclesiastical persons, . . . death unto Cattell, the exile of a great King or Prince, imprisonments or death, hate betweene the Commons and the greater sort, mutuail
hates and differences, motions of great Oathes and horrible warres, man-
slaughters, fire, theevery, repines, and depopulations: untimely birthes,
Agues, Pestilences, hot infirmities, death and barrennesse of fruits, and
notable mutations, . . . thefts and robberies.

The Sun likewise shall be Eclipsed on the second of October, . . . to
foreshew the death of some great King or Prince, seditions, warres, famine,
and Pestilence, . . . greevous sicknesses, diseases, . . . tempestuous and
most pernitious windes:[5]

Obviously one should not search for verbal parallels in Shakespeare's
passage and the prognostications of the time. Since every one of Edmund's and Gloster's "effects" of the "late eclipses" occurs subsequently

---

[4] Although the title-page gives the publication as "London, 1604," the book
contains a prognostication for 1603, indicating that it was originally printed (certainly written) before 1604. I cite the Folger Shakespeare Library copy.

[5] *Ibid.*, pp. 8–12, 3–4.

*in the play,* it would be a remarkable coincidence indeed if exact parallels should be found in any contemporary astrological pamphlet. But there is hardly any doubt that Shakespeare carefully adopted a *pattern* from such ephemeral literature; and by making the "effects" suit his plot, fashioned the astrologer's material into something quite his own. The conversation in *Lear* concerning the "late eclipses" stands out as incomparable literary dialogue as well as a harbinger of the subsequent action of the play; it must have appeared especially subtle and effective in being concerned with an actual topic of the times in which many people were vitally interested and concerning which some doubtless had grave misgivings. Furthermore, the argument that "these late eclipses" shows *Lear* to have been written after the eclipses of September and October, 1605, is somewhat weakened when we consider that prognostications concerning them were on the London bookstalls in 1604 or earlier.

There were also other eclipses prior to 1605 to which Shakespeare could have alluded. Visible in London were eclipses of the sun in 1598 and 1601, and several eclipses of the moon almost every year from 1598 onward.[6] It is not unreasonable to suppose, of course, that Shakespeare

[6] The best authorities by which to determine the occurrence, visibility, and length of time of eclipses are Th. Ritter von Oppolzer, *Canon der Finsternisse* . . . (Wien, 1887), Band 58, and J. Fr. Schroeter, *Sonnenfinsternisse von 600 bis 1800 N. Chr., mit 300 karten* (Kristiana, 1923). A neglect to examine carefully such records as these has led some scholars to make unwarranted conclusions regarding eclipses and their importance. For instance, O. F. Emerson, "Shakespeare's Sonneteering," *SP,* xx (1923), 111–136, dated *Sonnet 107* as of 1595 or 1596 because (he stated, p. 133) other than the total eclipse of the moon on April 14, 1595 "no other eclipse could have been seen there between December 20, 1591 and the beginning of 1599." As a matter of fact, there were lunar eclipses clearly visible in London in 1596 and 1598, as Oppolzer (pp. 367–368) will show.

The solar eclipses visible in London throughout Shakespeare's lifetime were not very numerous, occurring (according to Schroeter, pp. 10, 149–151, cxix–cxxii) as follows (Gregorian Calendar):

| | | |
|---|---|---|
| March 7, 1598 | 10:20 A.M. | Total |
| December 24, 1601 | 1:01 P.M. | Partial |
| October 12, 1605 | 1:08 P.M. | Total |

There were solar eclipses in Europe also in 1590, 1594, 1596, 1600, and 1610, but Schroeter's charts of the paths of these eclipses show clearly that only the three listed above were visible in England. If Shakespeare always remained in England, he never saw an eclipse of the sun until 1598—one lasting for more than two hours, and unusually conspicuous because it was total.

might have referred in *King Lear* to the eclipse of the sun in 1601 and any one of the many eclipses of the moon from 1598 onward.[7] Since other evidence, however, seems to limit the date of composition of the play as between 1603 and the end of 1606, it is highly probable that the topical passage in *King Lear* alludes to the eclipses of 1605.

Of course, to suppose that when Shakespeare alludes to an eclipse there must actually be such a phenomenon in the sky or a printed prognostication before his eyes is to put a somewhat narrow limitation upon the dramatist's imagination. Yet it is especially notable that Shakespeare mentions eclipses in no play written prior to 1601, but that he alludes to them somewhat frequently thereafter: in *Hamlet* (1.i.113–125), *Othello* (v.ii.98–101), *King Lear* (1.ii.98–141), *Macbeth* (11.iv.1–10; 1v.i.27–28), and *Antony and Cleopatra* (111.xiii.154–156). Since the large majority of notable eclipses visible in England during Shakespeare's lifetime occurred from 1598 onward, it would seem that all of Shakespeare's allusions to eclipses might have been suggested by actual eclipses of the time.[8]

Let us not depart from this subject without considering more precisely what the astrological authorities had to say with regard to eclipses and how to make prognostications based upon them. These celestial phenomena, caused by a conjunction or opposition of the sun and moon, were either *solar* or *lunar*.[9] Predictions by means of them—we have probably already gathered—were concerned not so much with

---

[7] In fact, B. M. Ward (*LTLS*, 1933, pp. 878, 909; 1934, p. 12) stoutly maintains that *Lear* reflects the solar and lunar eclipses of 1598, and that the play was written in that year.

[8] I quickly point out that eclipses are alluded to in *Sonnets 35, 60,* and *107.* If one insists upon an "early" date for the composition of the *Sonnets,* then one may rightly maintain that Shakespeare's allusions to eclipses are about evenly distributed throughout his works chronologically. But until we are better informed than we are now concerning the time of composition of the *Sonnets,* I will let the above analysis stand.

[9] A *solar* eclipse is one in which the moon stands immediately between the earth and the sun and thus obscures the light of the sun as well as the sun itself. It is caused when the sun and moon are in conjunction near one of the nodes at which the orbits of the earth and the moon intersect. A *lunar* eclipse is one in which the earth comes between the sun and the moon, depriving the moon of its illumination from the sun but not obscuring the moon's visibility as a dark and shadowy object. It occurs when the sun and moon are in opposition close to the moon's nodes.

ordinary individuals as with general events affecting large masses of people and large areas of territory—cities, districts, nations. They were utilized by the astrologers to prognosticate wars, pestilence, famine, drought, earthquakes, innundations, conflagrations, and the deaths of potentates and other great ones. When we delve into the astrologer's lore, we discover that the prognostication depended upon much more than simply the conjunction or opposition of the sun and moon. Indeed, the procedure required for predicting accurately the events that should follow an eclipse was a complicated business, as we shall see.

The known territory of the inhabited earth was divided by Claudius Ptolemy and other ancient scientists into four parts, each governed by one of the four triplicities (or groups of signs) of the zodiac.[10] That is to say, Europe is ruled over by the triplicity composed of Aries, Leo, and Sagittarius, and by the lords of that triplicity, Jupiter and Mars. Northern Asia is governed by Gemini, Libra, and Aquarius, whose lords are Jupiter and Saturn; Southern Asia, by Taurus, Virgo, Capricorn, Venus, and Saturn; Africa, by Cancer, Scorpio, Pisces, Mars, and Venus. Subdivisions of each of these major parts of the earth are likewise under the government of specific signs and planets. Britain, Galatia and Germany are governed particularly by Aries and Mars; Italy, Sicily, and Gaul are governed by Leo and the sun; Tuscany, Celtica, and Spain, by Sagittarius and Jupiter; and so on. Such data were basically necessary for determining the locality which the events following an eclipse would affect.

In predicting the results of an eclipse, the astrologer would first consult his ephemerides (tables of the daily positions of the planets in the zodiac) and cast a horoscope for the exact moment when the eclipse is to occur.[11] A horoscope (a figure or map of the heavens) is represented by a circle with a diameter drawn through it horizontally to represent the "eastern horizon" and the "western horizon," and with another

[10] *Quadripartitum,* trans. J. M. Ashmand (London, 1822; Chicago, 1936), Bk. II, chs. i–x, pp. 40–63 (esp. ch. iii). Cf. also Jerome Cardan's aphorisms relating to eclipses and comets in *Anima Astrologiae* (ed. William Lilly, London, 1675, 1886), pp. 100–101.

[11] Even in the fourteenth century, the Alphonsine and other astronomical tables allowed eclipses or any other planetary positions to be ascertained many years before the event took place. Cf. Johnstone Parr, "Astronomical Dating for Some of Lydgate's Poems," *PMLA,* XLVII (1952), 258; or Lynn Thorndike, *A History of Magic and Experimental Science* (New York, 1934), vols. III and IV, *passim.*

diameter drawn vertically through the center of the circle to represent
the meridian. Each of the four quadrants thus made are further divided into three equal parts by other diameters, making twelve equal
sections in all, forming what are known as the twelve "houses" of the
horoscope. Of these the first, fourth, seventh, and tenth—counting
counter-clockwise from the eastern horizon (on the left)—are called
"angles." The topmost part of such a figure (the tenth house) represents the "mid-heaven." The constantly revolving signs of the zodiac
are represented as passing in succession clockwise through all of these
houses, and the planets with them, one of the twelve signs of the zodiac
being in one of the houses at any given moment. Such a drawing gives
an adequately pictorial representation of the heavens at any given time.
(See the figure on page 105.)

Having erected such a figure, the astrologer would notice where in
the horoscope—particularly in what sign of the zodiac and what house
of the horoscope—the conjunction or opposition of the sun and moon
takes place. This "ecliptical place" in the zodiac foreshadows that the
coming events will fall upon those countries, cities, or districts under
the government of that zodiacal sign—England, for example, if the
eclipse occurs in Aries.[12] He next observed the length of time of the
obscuration, because the effect of the eclipse would last as many years
(if the eclipse is solar) or as many months (if the eclipse is lunar) as
the eclipse lasts hours. The position of the ecliptical place with respect
to the "angles" of the horoscope would determine when the effect
would begin as well as the time of its greatest intensity. For example,
Ptolemy stated that if the ecliptical place be near the eastern horizon,
the effect will begin in the first four months after the eclipse occurs,
and its greatest intensity will take place in the first third of its duration; if the ecliptical place be near the mid-heaven, the effect will begin
in the second four months and be most intense in the second third of

---

[12] The various complexities of all the astrological manipulations make it necessary that I state here only the very basic regulations in the simplest case
imaginable. In predicting for a particular city, for example, one considers the
transits of the sun and moon in the zodiac at the time the city was founded; and
if this date of the founding of the metropolis were not ascertainable, the mid-
heaven in the natal horoscope of the reigning king or other chief magistrate is to
be considered—all juxtaposed in a precise but most complex fashion with the
present horoscope for the actual eclipse.

its duration; and if the ecliptical place be near the western horizon, the effect will begin in the third four months and be most intense in the last third of its duration.[13]

Various items in such a horoscope are said to be in "dominion"—or have an especial role to play—in ascertaining the events brought about by the eclipse. Should the eclipse occur in Aries, for example, the planet in chief dominion would be Mars, the planet which generally governs Aries. The sign of the zodiac in which Mars is posited at the time of the eclipse would co-operate with Aries in regulating the coming events. Other items generally in dominion are the sign (and the planet governing the sign) on the angle preceding the ecliptical place, the sign (and the planet governing the sign) on the angle following the ecliptical place, and the brightest of the fixed stars during the eclipse.[14]

Having made such observations and wishing to predict what class of people, animals, or institutions would be most affected by the eclipse, the astrologer noted the astrological nature of the signs of the zodiac in dominion. If the signs were of human shape (Gemini, Virgo, Aquarius), the effects would fall upon the human race; if the signs were of tame beasts (Aries, Taurus, Capricorn), the effects would be inflicted upon domesticated animals; if the signs were of creatures that swim (Cancer, Pisces), the effects would be felt by marine animals and those who navigate ships. Equinoctial signs (Aries and Libra) indicated events likely to happen in ecclesiastical matters; tropical signs (Cancer and Capricorn), events in political affairs; fixed signs (Taurus, Leo, Scorpio, Aquarius), events concerning institutions and buildings; bicorporeal signs (Gemini, Virgo, Sagittarius, Pisces), events affecting princes and subjects. If these ruling signs were in the "east" of the horoscope, they affected fruits and seeds, incipient institutions, and the young; if in the mid-heaven, kings, princes, ecclesiastics, the middle-

---

[13] Ptolemy, *op. cit.*, Bk. ii, ch. vi, p. 54.

[14] *Ibid.*, Bk. ii, ch. viii, p. 55. Ptolemy observes, however: "If one planet have more numerous claims than any other to the place of the eclipse, as well as to that of the preceding angle, being in the immediate vicinity of those places, and having more rights over other places connected with them by configuration; . . . in such a case only that single planet is entitled to dominion. But if the lord of the eclipse and the lord of the angle preceding it be not identical, then those two planets which have most connections with each place are to be noted [as having dominion]." *Ibid.*, ii.viii.55–56.

aged; if in the "west," laws, old things, and persons about to die.[15] And so on and on.

The character of the events themselves the astrologer gathered from the nature of the planet which controls the ecliptical place, and from their relative admixture should two or more planets be thus in dominion. If Mars is the sole or chief governor in dominion during an eclipse, says Ptolemy:

He causes such mischief and destruction as are concomitant with dryness. And, among mankind, foreign wars will be excited, accompanied with intestine divisions, captivity, slaughter, insurrections of people, and wrath of princes against their subjects; together with sudden and untimely death. Feverish disorders, tertian agues, and haemorrhages will take place, and will be rapidly followed by painful death, carrying off chiefly youthful persons; and conflagrations, murder, impiety, every infraction of the law, adultery, rape, robbery, and all kinds of violence will be practised. The atmosphere will be parched by hot, pestilential, and blasting winds, accompanied by drought, lightnings, and fires emitted from the sky. At sea, ships will be suddenly wrecked, . . . Rivers will fail, springs will be dried up, . . . All the creatures and productions of the earth adapted to the use of man, whether beasts, grain, or fruits, will be damaged or destroyed by excessive heat, by storms or thunder and lightning, or by violent winds; and whatever has been deposited in store will be destroyed or injured by fire, or by heat.[16]

Saturn's influence was also evil, promoting disasters concomitant with cold, lingering diseases, exile, poverty, frequent deaths among the aged, unwholesome and gloomy atmosphere, hail and snow-storms, floods, tempests, disastrous voyages and shipwrecks, innundations, blight, famine, and "a general mass of evils, griefs, and alarms." Mercury in dominion promoted industry and skill in business, but also many thievish propensities, robberies, and plots of treachery; and if configurated with a malefic planet, calamities in navigation, dry and parching diseases, changes in religion, in affairs of government, manners, customs, and laws.[17] Not all eclipses, however, produced such violent and devastating effects. If a benefic planet such as Jupiter or Venus were in sole dominion, benevolent and harmonious events would ensue; for Ptolemy says:

[15] *Ibid.*, II.viii.pp.56–57.
[16] *Ibid.*, II.ix.pp.59–60.
[17] *Ibid.*, II.ix.pp.58–60.

Venus, alone in dominion, geneally produces the same [good] effects as Jupiter, yet with greater suavity and more agreeably. Glory, honour, and joy will attend mankind; happy marriages will be contracted, and the fortunate pairs will be blessed with numerous children. Every undertaking will proceed prosperously, wealth will increase, and the conduct of human life will be altogether pure, simple, and pious; due reverence being paid to all holy and sacred institutions, and harmony subsisting between princes and their subjects. The weather also will be of a favorable temperature, cooled by moistening breezes; the air altogether pure and salubrious, frequently refreshed by fertilizing showers. Voyages will be performed in safety, and be attended by success and profit. Rivers will receive their adequate supply of waters; and all things valuable and useful to mankind, whether animal or vegetable, will abundantly thrive and multiply.[18]

Such is a brief and simple account of the complicated manifestations which the "sectary astronomical" painstakingly wrought to make predictions based on eclipses of the sun and moon. Edmund might scoff at such activity as sheer duplicity, but his sarcasm apparently had little effect upon a host of such astrologers whose predictions were published and apparently read avidly throughout the sixteenth and seventeenth centuries.[19]

[18] *Ibid.*, ii.ix.p.60.
[19] The first portion of this chapter appeared in the *Shakespeare Association Bulletin*, xx (1945), 46–48.

## CHAPTER EIGHT

# EDMUND'S BIRTH UNDER
# URSA MAJOR

THE ONLY natal horoscope in Shakespeare's plays which has any "technical" significance is Edmund's nativity in *King Lear*. Nonchalantly and scoffingly Edmund tells us:

My father compounded with my mother under the Dragon's Tail, and my nativity was under Ursa Major; so that it follows I am rough and lecherous. Fut! I should have been that I am, had the maidenliest star in the firmament twinckled on my bastardizing.[1]

We need not dwell upon that item in the horoscope known as the Dragon's Tail; many editors have noted its sinister influence.[2] But Edmund's statement that his "nativity was under Ursa Major" and the conclusion that this configuration supposedly made him "rough and lecherous" has been ignored by all critics of the play.[3]

Ursa Major (known also as the Great Bear or the Big Dipper) is a group of fixed stars north of the zodiac whose astrological nature was reckoned as that of the planets Mars and Venus, with Mars predominating. Claudius Ptolemy, undoubtedly in the Renaissance the supreme authority in astrological matters, writes:

The constellations north of the zodiac have their respective influences,

---

[1] I.ii.121–125.

[2] We should observe, however, that Edmund does not say that the Dragon's Tail is in his horoscope, but simply that his father and mother "compounded" under the Dragon's Tail—or at a particularly evil time.

[3] The one exception is E. B. Knobel, "Astrology and Astronomy," in *Shakespeare's England* (Oxford, 1916, 1932), I, 459, who writes: "All the stars in Ursa Major were reckoned to be of the nature of Mars, who was 'choleric and fiery, a lover of slaughter and quarrels, murder, a traitor of turbulent spirit, perjured, and obscene.'" Although he cites no reference, Mr. Knobel is quoting from William Lilly's *Christian Astrology* (London, 1647; reprinted, 1939), pp. 40–41; and his statement that Ursa Major was governed by Mars alone is inaccurate.

analogous to those of the planets. . . . *Ursa Major* is like Mars, but the nebula under the tail resembles . . . Venus in its influence.[4]

If we consult the works of the astrological authorities, we discover that these two planets which governed Ursa Major produced a character remarkably similar to that of Edmund.

Richard Saunders, in a huge compendium which reports a host of Renaissance physiognomists and astrologers, specifically calls the Martial man "rough." Says he:

Those who are born Martial and under Aries are red or flaxen hair'd, a rough sort of people, rude and invincible; . . .[5]

Henry Cornelius Agrippa describes the Martial man similarly: "A sour, fierce, cruel, angry, rough countenance and gesture are ascribed to Mars."[6] And Ptolemy would ascribe many particulars of Edmund's character to the dominant influence of the war-planet:

Mars alone having dominion of the mind, and placed with glory, makes men . . . irascible, warlike, versatile, powerful in intellect, daring, bold, . . . obstinate, . . . self-confident, contemptuous, . . . tyrannical; but, posited ingloriously, he makes men cruel, mischievous, sanguinary, tumultuous, . . . rapacious, pitiless, familiar with crime, restless, . . . hostile to their families, and infidels in religion.[7]

As we have seen, the constellation of Ursa Major exerted the *combined* influences of Mars and Venus. The astrologers do not leave us in doubt as to the dispensations of such a configuration. Ptolemy continues:

[4] *Tetrabiblos sive Quadripartitum,* trans. J. M. Ashmand (London, 1822; Chicago, 1936), Bk. I, ch. x, p. 19. Many editions of Ptolemy's *Quadripartitum* were published in the sixteenth century: in 1533, 1535, 1541, 1551, 1554, 1559, 1581, etc.

[5] *Physiognomie, Chiromantie, Metoposcopie* (London, 1653), p. 157. At the beginning of this work, Saunders lists almost two hundred authors as his authorities.

[6] *De occulta philosophia, or Three Books of Occult Philosophy or Magic,* ed. W. F. Whitehead (New York, 1897), Bk. I, ch. lii, p. 156.

[7] *Op. cit.,* Bk. III, ch. xviii, p. 112. Similar statements may be found in Claudius Dariot's *A Briefe . . . Introduction to the Astrological Judgement of the Starres,* trans. Fabian Withers (London, 1583, 1591, 1598), sig. D3r; John Indagine's *Briefe Introductions unto . . . Natural Astrology,* trans. Fabian Withers (London, 1575, 1598), sigs. P1v, P2r; Augier Ferrier's *A Learned Astronomical Discourse of the Judgement of Nativities,* trans. Thomas Kelway (London, 1593), p. 14. (Copies I use are those of the Folger Shakespeare Library.)

Should Mars be conciliated with Venus, and . . . if he have an inglorious position when thus conciliated, he makes men overbearing, lascivious, sordid, opprobrious, adulterous, mischievous, liars, fabricators of deceit, cheats of their own families as well as others, eager in desire, . . . debauchers of wives and virgins, daring, impetuous, ungovernable, treacherous, faithless, dangerous, . . .[8]

And Albohazen Haly, chief representative of the Arabian astrologers, agrees:

If Mars is in harmony with Venus and in a good position, they create a native who . . . loves a vicious and depraved life. Such a native . . . is a reveler, . . . and has unlawful and sinful relations with the opposite sex; he is . . . a mocker and a deceiver, . . . easily angered. But if these planets are in positions opposite to that of which we have spoken, they make the native . . . meritricious, a dishonorer, a teller of lies, a deceiver of friends and others; successful in satisfying his desires, seducing and corrupting good women and virgins, wise in perpetrating frauds and betrayals. He is a perjurer, a scoffer and reviler, a reprobate in habits and thought, busily engaged in conceiving corrupt acts and in the practice of abominable fornication.[9]

It seems that almost any relationship between Mars and Venus would produce similarly deplorable results, for John Taisnier remarks that if Mars be even in the "house" of Venus (*i.e.,* in Taurus or Libra),

the native shall be voluptuous and a fornicator, perpetrating wickedness with women of his own blood, becoming guilty of incest, or committing adultery with women whom he has seduced by promises of marriage; . . .[10]

Thus the planet Mars (whose influence predominates in Ursa Major) is a malicious worker of evil, particularly when he mingles his influence with that of Venus (who also influences through Ursa Major). There is certainly no doubt that the astrological authorities would presage that one born under the influence of Ursa Major would be "rough and lecherous," and destined to become a villain of the first order.

[8] Ptolemy, *loc. cit.*

[9] *Liber completus in judiciis astrorum* (Venice, 1485, 1531; Basle, 1551, 1571); cited by Ioannes Baptista Porta, *Coelestis physiognomoniae libri sex* (Rothomagi, 1650; published also in 1603), p. 77.

[10] *Absolvtissimae Chyromantiae Libri Octo* (Cologne, 1563), p. 615; cited by Walter Clyde Curry, *Chaucer and the Mediaeval Sciences* (New York, 1926), p. 101.

Now Edmund's career shows him to be in large measure the living embodiment of astral influences exerted by the malignant constellation of Ursa Major. He is recognized immediately as the villain of the play after his first soliloquy, in which he informs us of his religious infidelity, his audacious independence, and his "invention" whereby he shall dupe his legitimate brother out of the latter's inheritance. As he pursues his plan of maliciously playing upon Gloster's credulity, we see Edmund's scoffing and contentious attitude toward his old father's belief that the recent eclipses portend no good for the kingdom. His complete independence, egotism, and religious infidelity are seen again in his belittling remarks about astrology, a science in which Lear, Kent, and Gloster all had faith.[11] His treachery and his martial lack of sympathy are fully exhibited by his deliberate betrayal of his father into the hands of those who pluck out the old man's eyes and send him stumbling off to Dover. His skill in devising deceits and frauds is well attested by the manner in which (Iago-like and in the fashion of a professional criminal) he dupes both Gloster and Edgar. But he is no coward; indeed, he possesses an unusual amount of military prowess, valor, courage, and strength of will. It is he who leads the "powers" of Albany and Regan, wins the battle against the invading French army, gives orders as to what should be done with the captives. He is bold enough to defy Albany and courageous enough to accept at once the challenge from Edgar.[12] Doubtless the predominance of Mars in his nativity is responsible for such martial—such "rough"—qualities. For Edmund is, like the Martial man, a purposeful adventurer—determined to seize first his brother's possessions and then (through deceitful and unscrupulous conciliation with Goneril or Regan) the crown. Also like the Martial man (to use Professor Bradley's phrasing), "he regards men and women, with their virtues and vices, together with the bonds of kinship, friendship, or allegiance, merely as hindrances or helps to his end." [13]

The planet Venus asserts her influence in Edmund's nativity also,

[11] Cf. Hardin Craig, "The Ethics of *King Lear*," *PQ,* IV (1925), 97–109, and his *Shakespeare* (New York, 1932), p. 851. Professor Craig maintains that "Edmund's denial of planetary influence must be set down as a sort of religious infidelity."

[12] v.iii.41 ff.

[13] A. C. Bradley, *Shakespearean Tragedy* (London, 1904, 1920), p. 301.

for there is no question but that he is (as Shakespeare tells us) "lecherous." We learn of Edmund's adulterous proclivities when he accom-
panies Goneril from Gloster's castle to her own.[14] And it is not long
thereafter that we find Regan suspicious of his having been abed with
sister Goneril.[15] Such amorous depravity is indeed the sort attributed to
the influence of Venus in conjunction with Mars; and to this astral
configuration might also be attributed Edmund's nonchalance and
faithlessness behind his frank confession:

> To both these sisters have I sworn my love;
> ·  ·  ·  ·  ·  ·  ·  ·  ·  ·  ·  ·  ·  ·  ·  ·
> Which of them shall I take?
> Both? one? or neither? [16]

At all events, an Elizabethan audience which perceived that Edmund
was born under the "rough and lecherous" constellation of Ursa Major
would have strongly suspected him sooner or later to "compound"
with such women of the play as were assailable.

So, it seems to me, did Edmund appear to an Elizabethan audience:
a Martial man with strong Venerian proclivities, because of the predominance of Ursa Major in his natal horoscope. And if this evil configuration appeared to the Elizabethans in any measure responsible for
Edmund's preoccupation with fraud, deceit, perjury, contemptuous-
ness, religious infidelity, and lechery, perhaps we need no longer wonder with Professor Bradley [17] why it is that "a man so young as Edmund
can have a nature so bad." [18]

[14] iv.ii.
[15] iv.v.19 ff; iv.vi.261 ff.
[16] v.i.55–58.
[17] *Op. cit.,* p. 301.
[18] The materials in this chapter were first published as "Edmund's Nativity in
*King Lear," Shakespeare Association Bulletin,* xxi (1946), 181–185.

## CHAPTER NINE

# THE DUKE OF BYRON'S
# MALIGNANT NATIVITY

DOUBTLESS one of the most entertaining of Elizabethan plays on contemporary political events was George Chapman's presentation of the
downfall of the famous Duke of Byron, the favorite of King Henry of
Navarre whose behavior at last caused his sovereign to send him to the
executioner's block. Professor Parrott sees Byron's over-weening pride,
consummate ambition, and blind conceit of his own importance as the
dominant causes of the Duke's tragic end.[1] That Byron possessed these
disaster-provoking qualities no one can deny. But I should like to em-
phasize a factor in the Duke's catastrophe which Professor Parrott has
apparently ignored: namely, that to the Elizabethans the motivating
force in Byron's tragedy lay in large measure in his stars.[2] It is my
purpose also to present an adequate explanation of the dreadful *Caput
Algol* which the astrologer La Brosse finds in the Duke's natal horoscope.

Scholars of the Renaissance are now aware of the fact that even those
Elizabethans who distrusted astrologers had faith to some extent in the
power of the stars; that astral influence was intricately linked with the
objective psychology which passed for sober science in that day; and
that hundreds of testimonials in Elizabethan plays in favor of stellar
influence far outnumber the few expressions berating astrology as sheer

[1] *The Plays and Poems of George Chapman*, ed. Thomas Marc Parrott (London and New York, 1910), I, 591–598 (esp. pp. 593, 597–598). Cf. also Hardin
Craig, "Ethics in the Jacobean Drama: the Case of Chapman," in *Essays in Dramatic Literature* (Princeton, 1935), pp. 25–46, who emphasizes the Elizabethan
science and objective psychology in Chapman's plays but offers no specific reason
for Byron's catastrophe.

[2] For a similar treatment of the catastrophe in Marlowe's *Tamburlaine*, see
Chapter I.

quackery or a figment of the imagination.[3] Professor D. C. Allen, in
his excellent study of attitudes toward astrology in England during the
period, writes:

> My inference now is that everybody who lived during the Renaissance be-
> lieved to some extent in astrology. . . . None of the English opponents
> of astrology was willing to say that the stars were without influence; at
> most, they denied that the planets had the governing of the human will
> and that the influence of the stars could either be measured or predicted.
> . . . The astrological learning of the Elizabethan and Jacobean men of
> letters . . . indicates the popularity of this type of information among the
> ordinary citizens who were the writers' customers . . . [and] indicates a
> definite and widespread belief in the art. We can no longer say that it
> was accepted by only the credulous, the unenlightened, and the super-
> stitious. . . . The poets say that the stars do not control all things or that
> the influence of the stars may be altered; they do not deny that the stars
> are causes.[4]

It is not strange, therefore, to find that when Byron files his mind
with apprehensions of treason, and secretly leagues himself with
avowedly sworn enemies of the King who anticipate seizure of the
French throne, his mind misgives and he decides to have his horoscope
judged by an astrologer who lives nearby. As he hies to this "magician"
with intentions of probing his astral destiny, he says:

> I'll be resolved by a magician
> That dwells hereby, to whom I'll go disguis'd
> And show him my birth's figure, set before
> By one of his profession, of the which
> I'll crave his judgment, feigning I am sent
> From some great personage, whose nativity
> He wisheth should be censur'd by his skill.
> But on go my plots, be it good or ill.[5]

[3] Cf. D. C. Allen, *The Star-Crossed Renaissance* (Durham, North Carolina,
1941), *passim*: Willard Farnham, *The Mediaeval Heritage of Elizabethan
Tragedy* (Berkeley, California, 1936), 102 ff.; Lynn Thorndike, *A History of
Magic and Experimental Science* (New York, 1922–1941), vols. v and vi, *passim;*
Ruth L. Anderson, *Elizabethan Psychology in Shakespeare's Plays* (Iowa City,
Iowa, 1927); Lily B. Campbell, *Shakespeare's Tragic Heroes: Slaves of Passion*
(Cambridge, 1930).

[4] *Op. cit.*, pp. viii, 143–144, 181–182, 184.

[5] *Byron's Conspiracy*, iii.ii.287–294. All citations are from Parrott's edition,
*op. cit.*

The astrologer, however, is not deceived: he discovers the minute he looks at Byron's horoscope that the configuration of signs and planets thereon describes the very man before him. Moreover, his art is so precise that he correctly anticipates the very hour Byron visits him to be particularly malignant to his own welfare; for he comments immediately prior to Byron's entrance:

> This hour by all rules of astrology
> Is dangerous to my person, if not deadly.
> How hapless is our knowledge to foretell,
> And not be able to prevent a mischief:
> O the strange difference 'twixt us and the stars;
> They work with inclinations strong and fatal,
> And nothing know; and we know all their working,
> And nought can do, or nothing can prevent! [6]

Byron enters, *"disguised like a Carrier of Letters,"* and the following conversation ensues:

> Byron: I would entreat you, for some crowns I bring,
> To give your judgment of this figure cast,
> To know, by his nativity there seen,
> What sort of end the person shall endure
> Who sent me to you and whose birth it is.
> La Brosse: I'll herein do my best in your desire;
> *[He contemplates the figure]*
> The man is raised out of good descent,
> And nothing older than yourself, I think;
> It is not you?
> Byron: I will not tell you that:
> But tell me on what end he shall arrive.
> La Brosse: My son, I see that he, whose end is cast
> In this set figure, is of noble parts,
> And by his military valour rais'd
> To princely honours, and may be a king;
> But that I see a *Caput Algol* here
> That hinders it, I fear.
> Byron: A *Caput Algol?*
> What's that, I pray?
> La Brosse: Forbear to ask me, son;
> You bid me speak what fear bids me conceal.
> . . . . . . . . . . . . . . . . .
> You'll rather wish you had been ignorant,

[6] III.iii.1–8.

> Than be instructed in a thing so ill.
>
> Byron:  . . . do not urge me to enforce
> What I would freely know; . . .
>
>                                 I'll lay thy brain
> Here scatter'd at my feet and seek in that
> What safely thou must utter with thy tongue,
> . . . Be free, and speak the worst.
>
> La Brosse: Then briefly this: the man hath lately done
> An action that will make him lose his head.

Thereupon Byron, in a rage, seizes the poor old man, trounces him almost to death, and exclaims:

> Pox of your halting humane knowledges;
>
> .   .   .   .   .   .   .   .   .   .   .   .   .   .
>
> Spite of the stars, and all astrology,
> I will not lose my head; or if I do
> A hundred thousand heads shall off before.
> I am a nobler substance than the stars,
> And shall the baser overrule the better?
> Or are they better, since they are the bigger?
> I have a will, and faculties of choice,
> To do, or not to do: and reason why
> I do, or not do this; the stars have none.
> They know not why they shine more than this taper,
> Nor how they work, nor what; I'll to my course.
> I'll piece-meal pull the frame of all my thoughts,
> And cast my will into another mould:
> And where are all your *Caput Algols* then?
> Your planets all, being underneath the earth
> At my nativity: what can they do?
> Malignant in aspects? in bloody houses?
> Wild fire consume them!
>
> .   .   .   .   .   .   .   .   .   .   .   .   .
>
> O that mine arms were wings, that I might fly,
> And pluck out of their hearts my destiny! [7]

[7] III.iii.38–127. About half of the conversation in this scene is taken from Chapman's source, Grimeston's *General Inventorie of the History of France* (London, 1607), pp. 993–994. Although Professor Parrott (p. 606) leads one to believe that the *entire* scene is taken over from this source, one notices that the speech by La Brosse preceding the interview and the speech by Byron at the end of the interview are not in Grimeston. Incidentally, Grimeston begins his account of the interview and Byron's horoscope with the following statement: "The second cause of his ruine was the alteration of his Fortune."

Byron may thus convince himself for the nonce that stellar influence and astrological precepts are mere twaddle and that a man's will and valor make him thus and thus; but, as La Brosse predicts, his life will be ended shortly by the stroke of the executioner's sword.

Now Byron tells us that all the planets in his horoscope are in "malignant aspects" and are "underneath the earth." Being in "malignant aspects" means in astrology that the planets are unfavorably situated in relation to one another.[8] And the astrologers are agreed that a planet's position "underneath the earth" (i. e., below the horizon or in the lower 180 degrees of the horoscope) is generally a very unfortunate place for a planet to be.[9] But the most significant item in the horoscope is the *Caput Algol* by which the astrologer so surely judged that Byron would lose his head.

Professor Parrott has explained only that the *Caput Algol* is "an astrological term" designating a fixed star in the head of Medusa, which is represented in the constellation of Perseus (a group of northern stars between Taurus and Cassiopeia); but he has added the speculation that "there is probably a special connection here between the Medusa's head, cut off by Perseus, and Byron's which, as La Brosse foresaw, was to fall beneath the executioner's sword." [10] Professor Parrott's guess was shrewd, for everyone learned in astrological lore in Chapman's day knew that a malignant *Caput Algol* in one's horoscope presaged one's decapitation. In one of the most popular of the cheap booklets on astrology in the sixteenth century, *The Compost of Ptholomaeus,* we find the following:

Under the xxii degree of Taurus ryseth a sterre fixed of the first magnytude that Astronomers call Perseus sone of Jupiter that smote the heed of

---

[8] The "bloody houses" Byron mentions are not orthodox astrological terms; we must assign them to Chapman's poetic fancy. Cf. Parrott's note: ". . . since certain positions [of the planets] portended a bloody or violent death, hence *bloody houses."*

[9] Cf. Claudius Dariot, *A Briefe Introduction to the Astrologicall Judgement of the Starres,* trans. Fabian Withers (London, 1598), sig. H2r; Augier Ferrier, *A Learned Astronomical Discourse of the Judgement of Nativities,* trans. Thomas Kelway (London, 1593), p. 8; William Lilly, *Christian Astrology* (London, 1647), ed. Zadkiel (London, 1939), p. 165. Lilly reports: "The Lord of the Ascendant under the Earth and in ill aspect to the lord of the eighth house" is one of the "Arguments of Death." Cf. figure, p. 105.

[10] *Op. cit.,* p. 606.

Meduse. . . . Ptholomaeus and other Astronomyers say that whan Mars is conjoined with this sterre they that ben borne under the constellacyon shall have theyr heedes smyten of if God shape not remedy.[11]

Augier Ferrier, whose complete and authoritative textbook on astrology was translated and published in London in 1593, records:

The Sunne, or the Moone, or the Lord of the Ascendant, joyned with Mars, have right in one fixed starre, which the Astrologers call the head of Meduse or otherwise the head of the divel, maketh him by the hand of the Executioner to leese his head.[12]

Jerome Cardan, perhaps the Renaissance's most renowned astrologer, writes in his *De Supplemento Almanack*:

Cui [ascenderit] caput Algol infortunatur, accidet capitis periculum: si fortunabitur, acquiret gladiis super homines potestatem.[13]

William Lilly, the foremost professional astrologer of seventeenth-century London, lists the following as one of the "Arguments of Death":

the lord of the ascendant . . . being conjoined with *Aldebaran, Antares, Caput Algol,* or other violent fixed stars.[14]

In fact, Lilly found Mars approaching *Caput Algol* in the horoscope of King Charles I in a judgment of the king's horoscope made two years before that monarch was beheaded. Judged Lilly: "Luna is with *Antares,* a violent fixed star . . . which is said to denote *violent death* . . . and Mars, approaching *Caput Algol,* which is said to denote *beheading,* might intimate that." [15] And Claudius Ptolemy, perhaps astrology's supreme spokesman, provided the source materials for the majority of astrologers thus:

[11] Page 32 r (Folger Library copy). For editions, see *STC*.
[12] *Op. cit.,* p. 25.
[13] *Cardani Opera Omnia* (Lyons, 1663), v, 589. Cf. also: "Cum caput algol peragravit Asiam minorem, & Graeciam, in annis ferme 400. destruxit eas provincias usque ad extremum, & desertas ac oppressas a Mahumethanis reddidit. Nunc autem inuasit Italiam, est enim perpendicularis super Apuliam & Neapolitanum regnum, utinam nobis nihil ferat nocumenti." *Ibid.,* p. 584.
[14] *Op. cit.,* p. 166.
[15] *Op. cit.,* p. 288. Lilly's text was published in 1647; King Charles was beheaded in 1649.

If Mars be in imperfect signs, or near the Gorgon (*Caput Medusae*) of Perseus, it will produce death by decapitation, or by mutilation of limbs.[16]

If the Sun be found with the Gorgon's head (*Caput Medusae*), and not aspected by any benefic star, and if there be no benefic present in the eighth [house of the horoscope], and the lord of the conditionary luminary be opposed to Mars, or in quartile to him, the native will be beheaded.[17]

All of these unfortunate conditions mentioned by Ptolemy may be satisfied in Byron's nativity. We may suppose from La Brosse's remarks upon the decapitation that either Sol or Mars or Luna (or perhaps the "lord" of Byron's ascendant) is near the *Caput Algol*. This configuration is "not aspected by any benefic star" because Byron tells us that all the planetary aspects in his horoscope are "malignant." There can be "no benefic in the eighth" house of the horoscope, for that house is *above* the occidental horizon and all Byron's planets are admittedly *below*. And since all his planets are within the lower 180 degrees of the horoscope, the "lord of the conditionary luminary" can be in quartile aspect to Mars (i.e., at a distance of 90 degrees from that planet). Furthermore, should the conjunction of the *Caput Algol* and Byron's "Lord of the Ascendant" have been precisely under the earth (i.e., in the fourth house of the horoscope), the configuration would have been particularly significant since the fourth house is the portion of the horoscope representing "the *end* of all things." [18] We cannot assume, of course, that such a horoscope (with a malignant *Caput Algol* in the fourth house) is precisely what Chapman had in mind. But we can have no doubt that in the analysis of Byron's nativity La Brosse knew his astrological business according to the authorities,[19]

---

[16] *Tetrabiblos or Quadripartitum*, trans. J. M. Ashmand (London, 1822; Chicago, 1936), Bk. iv, ch. ix, p. 136. The Latin text as found in Francisco Junctinus' *Speculum Astrologiae* (Basle, 1581), I, 427, reads: "At si in abscissis membra vel imperfectarum formarum signis, seu in cathenae capite cum eis domino Perseo fuerit, capitis, sive membrorum abscissione migrabit."

[17] Ptolemy's *Centiloquium* LXXIII (appended to Ashmand, *op. cit.*). The Latin in Junctinus' edition (*op. cit.,* pp. 476, 839) reads: "Sol ubi repertus fuerit cum capite Gorgonis, sive Medusae, si neque aspicitur a benefica stella, neque benefica octavo loco praeest, dominusque conditionarii luminaris Marti opponitur, aut eum è quadrangulo pèrcutit, ei qui natus, caput truncabitur."

[18] Lilly, *op. cit.,* p. 30.

[19] La Brosse's delineation of Byron's horoscope is not at all the facetious and satirical treatment found in Beaumont and Fletcher's *The Bloody Brother* (iv.ii),

and that those in the audience who considered astrology a science to be reckoned with were not particularly astonished when Byron fulfilled his astral destiny by being led to the executioner's block.

Now Byron is undoubtedly that type of Renaissance man who believed that a strong and wise man may overrule his stars. We have noticed his scorn of their powers at the end of his conference with La Brosse. But we may also notice that throughout the play he never allows himself to forget for long that the stars are exercising their power upon him. He is reported to have told Queen Elizabeth that the stars

> are divine books to us, and are read
> By understanders only, the true objects
> And chief companions of the truest men; [20]

He cries to the henchmen who come to take him into custody:

> And take away my sword;
> A proper point of force; ye had as good
> Have robb'd me of my soul, slaves of my stars
> Partial and bloody! O that in mine eyes
> Were all the sorcerous poison of my woes
> That I might witch ye headlong from your height,
> And trample out your execrable light. [21]

When his execution draws near, his remarks ever revert to the influence of his stars:

> My envious stars cannot deny me this,
> That I may make my judges witnesses; [22]

> My courage raised me,
> For the dear price of five and thirty scars,
> And that hath ruin'd me, I thank my stars. [23]

> I'll break my blood's high billows 'gainst my stars. [24]

And in his last speech, at the execution block, he continues to blame

---

where a set of acknowledged rogues learnedly offer the client an incongruous analysis of a horoscope by bandying back and forth almost every abstruse term in the astrological dictionary. Incidentally, one of the lines so bandied about is "And *Caput Algol* in the house of Death."

[20] *Byron's Conspiracy*, iv.i.217–219.

[21] *Byron's Tragedy*, iv.ii.280–286.

[22] *Ibid.*, v.ii.203–204.      [23] *Ibid.*, v.iii.181–183.      [24] *Ibid.*, v.iv.20.

his fate upon his stars as he remonstrates to the witnesses that they should observe how the fateful celestial bodies designed his destiny:

> Fall on your knees then, statists, ere ye fall,
> That ye may rise again: knees bent too late
> Stick you in earth like statues: see in me
> How you are poured down from your clearest heavens.[25]

Thus is the significance of Byron's unfortunate horoscope dramatically and constantly brought to the attention of the audience.

I cannot agree with Professor Parrott that the scene between Byron and La Brosse is "an epic digression or episode." [26] It is, it seems to me, a highly dramatic scene in which the playwright has obviously made much of the stars as the motivating power behind Byron's catastrophe. I suggest that Chapman apparently rested content to blame the Duke's unfortunate end at least partly on his malignant natal horoscope.

How did the audience react to the play? Did the Elizabethan theatre-goer see in Byron's tragedy a conflict between "individual liberty" and "social order"? [27] Did they see Byron's pride, arrogance, ambition, and blind conceit as character deficiencies which spelled doom for their possessor? A few sitting in the gallery may have perceived these things; but the ordinary Elizabethan standing in the pit doubtless saw in Byron a man doomed by a malignant *Caput Algol*.[28]

[25] *Ibid.*, v.iv.253–256.
[26] *Op. cit.*, p. 596.
[27] *Ibid.*, p. 598.
[28] I thank the University of Alabama Research Committee for purchasing microfilm of several of the books used in preparing this chapter. The materials in it first appeared as "The Duke of Byron's Malignant *Caput Algol*," *SP*, XLIII (1946), 194–202.

## CHAPTER TEN

## PROGNOSTICATING VIOLENT DEATH

IN ALMOST all the plays of the Elizabethan and Jacobean dramatists one finds an abundance of astrological jargon used metaphorically and as sheer literary garnish, showing no particular knowledge of the complex technicalities of astrology. Occasionally, however, a Jacobean drama-tist's delineation of a horoscope involves such astrological technicalities that he and his audience must have fully appreciated the various mani-festations of horoscopy. Such is the case in John Webster's *The Duch-ess of Malfi.* My purpose in this chapter is to present an adequate ex-planation of the horoscope employed at one of the critical moments in this play.

At the beginning of the second act the widowed Duchess has already clandestinely married Antonio (the major-domos of her palace), is big with Antonio's child, and (by wearing loose-fitting gowns) has suc-ceeded in keeping the household of her palace from knowing of her pregnancy. On the night of the child's birth, Antonio plans a ruse to further keeping the secret: he announces that the Duchess' jewels have been stolen, and thereupon orders that the gates be shut and all mem-bers of the household confine themselves to their chambers for the night. This has no sooner been done than Antonio is informed that he is "the happy father of a sonne." He hurries off at once to cast the child's horoscope, or, as he says, to "set a figure for's Nativitie." [1] But

[1] II.ii.92. All citations from the play are from *The Complete Works of John Webster,* ed. F. L. Lucas (London, 1927), II. Professor Lucas (p. 151) is amused that Antonio, immediately after a lecture from Delio on superstition, should hurry away to cast a horoscope. But Webster apparently knew what recent re-search is beginning to clearly show: that in the early sixteenth century the chil-dren of a Duchess always had their horoscopes cast, and that this manifestation received virtually as much serious consideration as did the child's christening. Cf. Lynn Thorndike, *A History of Magic and Experimental Science* (New York,

in the process of this astrological manipulation, Antonio is approached by Bosolo, the spy of the Malfi brothers, who, upon hearing the Duchess' shrieks and suspecting all the while what is amiss, ignores the command that he remain in his lodgings. After an argument that almost ends in physical combat, Antonio warns him not to pass the door that leads to the Duchess' lodgings, and leaves. But in his excitement, he drops unknowingly the horoscope he has been casting. Bosolo, alone, retrieves it and discovers the Duchess' secret.

What's here? a childes Nativitie calculated! [Reads] *The Dutchess was deliver'd of a Sonne, 'tweene the hours twelve, and one, in the night: Anno Dom: 1504.* (that's this yeere) *decimo nono Decembris* (that's this night) *taken according to the Meridian of Malfy* (that's our Dutchesse: happy discovery!). *The Lord of the first house, being combust in the ascendant, signifies short life: and Mars being in a human signe, joyn'd to the taile of the Dragon, in the eight house, doth threaten a violent death;* Caetera non scrutantur.[2]

Then Bosolo hurries off to convey what he knows to the Malfi brothers, whose murderous wrath ultimately brings about the destruction of the Duchess and two of her base-blooded children by Antonio.

Professor Lucas' annotations on the terms used in this astrological passage are, in the main, correct.[3] He observes that *combust* is an astrological term meaning "burnt up"—that it refers to a planet's being unfortunately posited within $8\frac{1}{2}$ degrees of the sun, a position in which the planet's benign influence is all but destroyed. He points out that the *ascendant* is the sign of the zodiac rising (or "ascending") on the eastern horizon, and is therefore in the first of the twelve houses of the horoscope. He notices that the *human signs* of the zodiac are Gemini, Virgo, Sagittarius, and Aquarius, and that the *eighth house* of the horoscope is the malignant "House of Death" just as the first house is the "House of Life." He observes also that the *Dragon's Tail* is that point in the heavens where the moon crosses the sun's ecliptic in her descent into southern latitude, and he points out that the Dragon's Tail was regarded as exerting "a sinister influence." But Professor Lucas has not observed that Antonio's prognostications of "short life" and "a violent death" are, according to the astrological authorities, precisely

1923–1941), v, 159 ff.; Don Cameron Allen, *The Star-Crossed Renaissance* (Duke University Press, 1941), p. 52.

[2] II.iii.72–80.     [3] *Op. cit.,* II, 147, 153.

correct; that the information which Webster gives is enough to allow
us to cast at least a part of the horoscope, and conclude that it is a
purely hypothetical one craftily designed by Webster for his dramatic
purposes.

We may notice first that the horoscope is dated December 19, at
which time (Julian Calendar) the sun will be *in any year* approximately 7 degrees in Capricorn.[4] Now in order for the "lord of the first
house" in this horoscope to be within 8½ degrees of the sun in the first
house (or "combust in the ascendant"), Capricorn must be the sign in
the first house. Moreover, since the "lord" of a house is that planet
which "rules" the sign in the house, and since Saturn is judged by all
astrologers to be the ruler of Capricorn, then Saturn must be in combustion in the first house. Antonio has further calculated that in the
eighth house Mars is in conjunction with the Dragon's Tail in a
human sign. If Capricorn is in the first house, the human sign in this
case must be Virgo.[5] This, then, is the horoscope about which Antonio
has had time only to write:

*The Lord of the first house, being combust in the ascendant, signifies short
life: and Mars being in a human signe, joyn'd to the taile of the Dragon, in
the eight house, doth threaten a violent death.*

An astrologer would be appalled indeed upon discovering such a set
of malignant configurations in the nativity of his client. Augier Ferrier,
whose particularly complete textbook of astrology was translated and
published in London in 1593, writes:

The Sunne in the first house maketh the chylde . . . most advanced of all
his bretheren. . . . [But] If the lord of the first house . . . bee unfortunate
[combust, for example] in the first house, the childe shall not live long.
. . . If the Dominator of the ascendant be burnde [i.e., combust] the child
shall dye before 9 daies be accomplished . . . (except when he is burned
in his owne house or exaltation).[6]

[4] See an Ephemeris for any year.

[5] Although a horoscope with Capricorn ascending requires that Leo govern
the eighth house, yet the revolution of the signs through the houses makes it possible that some degrees of Virgo (which, when Capricorn ascends, rules the ninth
house) actually rule a portion of the eighth house; and should Mars, in our case,
have just entered Virgo, his position in the horoscope would be in Virgo and in
the eighth house rather than in the ninth. See figure, p. 105.

[6] *A Learned Astronomical Discourse on the Judgement of Nativities*, trans.
Thomas Kelway (London, 1593), pp. 43, 49, 9. We may notice, in regard to the
last statement, that in our case Saturn *is* in his "owne house," Capricorn.

Under the caption of "Annotationes Universales" in the elaborate *Speculum Astrologiae* of Francisco Junctinus, we find:

Dominus primae domus in primae domo fortunatus, dat nato longam vitam. Infortunatus vero vel combustus significat vitam brevem.[7]

And William Lilly, foremost of the professional astrologers of seventeenth-century London, records some pertinent remarks:

If the lord of the ascendant be under the Sun's beams, or going to combustion, . . . judge that the native shall not be long lived, but is near some danger or misfortune. . . . Saturn [if "lord of the horoscope"] in conjunction with Sol signifies losses to the querent by fire, or by men in power, who persecute him, and confine him within the walls of a prison . . . ; and he is seldom healthy or of long life.[8]

Our astrologer would surely stroke his beard and look with grave misgivings upon Antonio's son's chances for a long life. He would be doubly disturbed when he glanced at the configuration in the eighth house: Mars in conjunction with the Dragon's Tail in a human sign. For Augier Ferrier records in his chapter "Of the Death" the following:

You must consider if there be any planet in the eighth house, for he is the significator of the Death. . . . If Mars be the Significator of death, . . . and be very evil disposed, it maketh him to be hanged and strangled, or smothered, or otherwise killed in his bedde, or on hys horse.

If the tayle of the Dragon bee joyned to the Significator of death, denotes poisons, venims, and violent medicines. Mars within the eighth, . . . the Lord of the ascendant unfortunate, witnesse violent death, by the shedding of blood or otherwise.

In the eighth house, Mars, out of his principal dignitie, signifieth hayste death, pestilence, impediment, slaughter, and other sorts of violent death. . . . The tayle of the Dragon (in the eighth house) denotes horrible death.[9]

Claudius Ptolemy, perhaps the supreme astrological authority, states:

Mars, if in signs of human form, . . . and contrary in condition [i.e.,

---

[7] (Lugduni, 1581), I, 379.

[8] *Christian Astrology* (London, 1647). I cite from Zadkiel's 1852 edition entitled *An Introduction to Astrology by William Lilly* (London, 1939), pp. 83, 317.

[9] Ferrier, *op. cit.*, pp. 24, 25, 46. Cf. also Lilly, *op. cit.*, p. 251: "The manner of death . . . is chiefly shewn by the lord of the 8th house, or any planet therein. . . . If evil planets be there, they shew violent death, or fevers, and long and painful illnesses; . . . The Dragon's Tail with the significator of death is very evil."

evilly aspected], will operate violent death, either in civil or foreign war, or by suicide.[10]

And Junctinus agrees:

Mars in octava domo, et in signo humano, aut in secunda facie Tauri, vel prima Leonis, ferro interiturum obnunciat.[11]

Thus we discover Antonio precisely accurate in his judgment of his son's natal horoscope.

Professor Lucas believes it "a curious piece of irony, whether intended by Webster or no" that the native of this horoscope is eventually the only member of the family to survive.[12] Indeed, one would ordinarily expect that a child with such an appalling malignancy in his horoscope would depart from this world speedily. Such is not the judgment, however, of the professional astrologers. William Lilly is particularly emphatic in instructing his readers to "avoid rash judgments, especially of death." Death, he continues,

should never be judged by one single testimony, however strong. And though the lord of the ascendant be going to combustion in the house of death, observe whether the moon, Jupiter, or Venus (or Mercury if well aspected and strong) throw any good aspect to the lord of the ascendant before he comes to perfect conjunction with Sol; for then either medicine or natural strength will contradict that malignant influence, or take off part of that misfortune. . . . Concerning the absolute time of death, I have found it best to be wary.[13]

In the play Antonio absconds with his first son and heir to escape the plots against them by the Duchess' brothers. Possibly (as Lilly would say) the little influence which a benevolent Jupiter or Venus (or even Mercury) can exert on the child's fortunes allows him to escape temporarily the fate of strangulation that his mother and his younger brother and sister experience; and possibly the Sun in his ascendant was responsible for his being thus (as Ferrier would presage) "advanced of all his bretheren." At any rate, we see young Antonio last at

[10] *Quadripartitum or Tetrabiblos,* trans. J. M. Ashmand (London, 1822; Chicago, 1935), Bk. IV, ch. ix. The Latin in Melanchthon's edition (Basileae, 1553) reads: "Mars autem cum Solem infaustum, aut Lunam quadrato adspectu aut opposito adspicit, in signis humanis significat neces in seditionibus civilibus, aut interficendos ab hostibus, aut sua manu."

[11] *Op. cit.,* p. 477.

[12] *Op. cit.,* II, 151.

[13] *Op. cit.,* p. 85.

the very end of the play, under the care of Antonio's old friend Delio, who, when he hears that Antonio has been murdered, turns to his friends and remarks:

> Let us . . . joyne our force
> To establish this yong hopefull Gentleman
> In's mothers right.[14]

The play thereupon closes, and we are left with the thought that attempts will be made to restore "this yong hopefull Gentleman" to his proper titles. But there will surely be difficulties. The Duchess had an elder son—her heir apparent—by her first husband (III.iii.82). Delio will have to utilize indeed a goodly "force" to establish Antonio's heir. In view of this consideration, who can say that malignant Mars, the Dragon's Tail, and a "combust" lord of the ascendant in young Antonio's natal horoscope will not at any moment turn him off violently as the astrologers would predict? Has not Webster deliberately given to the child a horoscope which will ultimately doom him to the same fate experienced by his father and mother and the other children of this tragically fated marriage?

In the main source of Webster's story, the twenty-third Novell in Painter's *Palace of Pleasure,* a horoscope is nowhere mentioned; nor is one to be found in any of the minor sources of the play that have been suggested. I once thought it likely that Webster secured the horoscope from some historical account of the Malfi family which scholars are not aware of as one of the playwright's sources—that is, the horoscope might be one that had actually been cast for Antonio's son on December 19, 1504, and then recorded in the Malfi family's history (as the Pirckheimers, for instance, recorded the horoscopes of various members of their family).[15] But this idea was immediately dispelled when I consulted the *Ephemerides* of Regiomontanus[16] and discovered that on December 19, 1504, Saturn was not in Capricorn but in Leo, and Mars was not in Virgo but in conjunction with the sun in Capricorn. In Webster's horoscope, the sun and Saturn must be in Capricorn, and Capricorn must be ascending; Mars must be in the eighth house, not

---

[14] v.v.135–138.

[15] Cf. Thorndike, *op. cit.,* v, 351–352.

[16] Johannes Muller von Konigsburg (Regiomontanus), *Ephemerides . . . ab 1504* (Venice, 1484). (Harvard Library copy.)

(as it actually was) conjoined with the sun in Capricorn. As a matter of fact, the *Ephemerides* shows that the configurations which Webster presents did not occur *at any time* during the early years of the sixteenth century.[17]

We may conclude, then, that Webster produced a purely hypothetical horoscope to suit the dramatic purposes of his play, that he selected with considerable care (possibly from Ferrier and Ptolemy) his particular configurations and the prognostications to result therefrom, and that he knew enough of the technicalities of horoscopy to give his remarks on young Antonio's nativity a considerable amount of "scientific" verisimilitude.[18]

[17] It is, of course, quite possible that Webster simply lifted the horoscope from one of the astrology texts of the sixteenth century which were replete with illustrative horoscopes and the nativities of famous personages; and, by merely changing its date to coincide with that of the Duchess' history, infused it into his play. With this idea in mind, I searched in vain through the fifth book of Luke Gaurico's *Tractatus astrologicus* (which contains forty-six horoscopes presaging violent death); the *De centum genituram* and all the other astrological treatises in volume v of Jerome Cardan's *Opera Omnia;* Rudolphus Goclenius' *Acroteleuticon astrologicum* (Francofurti, 1608); and Francisco Junctinus' *Speculum astrologiae* (which contains almost one thousand horoscopes).

[18] The author wishes to express his gratitude to the University of Alabama Research Committee for the purchase of microfilms of some of the rare books used in the preparation of this chapter. The materials in it first appeared as "The Horoscope in Webster's *The Duchess of Malfi*," PMLA, LX (1945), 760–765.

## CHAPTER ELEVEN

# CATCHING A THIEF AND FINDING STOLEN GOODS

OCCASIONALLY an Elizabethan or Jacobean dramatist's employment of a single and apparently casual reference presupposes on the part of the dramatist and audience a thorough acquaintance with the mysteries of some branch of astrology. As we read the play more than three centuries later, altogether too often an appreciation of this particular and interesting branch of a scientific system is lost to us. The dramatist's admirable economy of explanatory details implies an accurate knowledge of scientific principles about which in his own day it was unnecessary that he enter upon a full discussion, just as it is unnecessary today for a dramatist who mentions "suppressed desires" to stop the main business of his play and explain the principles of Freudian psychology. With this precept in mind, we may turn to an aspect of astrology at the finger-tips of many Elizabethans but little known to us: the planetary art of catching a thief and finding stolen goods.

In Robert Wilson's *Wily Beguiled,* when the heroine Lelia elopes with Churms, her father states the belief that runaways may be found by means of astrology; for he says:

> I'll go to Sophos, . . .
> Perhaps he hath some skill in hidden arts,
> Of planets course, or secret magic spells,
> To know where Lelia and that fox lies hid.
>                                                       (ll. 2406–10)

Another manifestation of this use of astrology to find lost or stolen property is referred to when the Conjuror in John Webster's *The White Devil* denounces the astrologers, his rivals in trade, as

> Fellowes indeed that onely live by stealth,
> Since they do merely lie about stolen goods.
>                                                       (ii.ii.16–17)

Then we recall (from the last chapter) that Antonio in Webster's *The Duchess of Malfi* announces as a ruse that the Duchess' jewels have been stolen, and that he orders the members of the household to be locked in their chambers for the night until an investigation and search can be made. When that night Antonio is casting the horoscope for the baby to whom the Duchess has secretly just given birth, the suspicious Bosola apprehends Antonio in the manipulation of this astrological endeavor. To explain what he is doing without revealing the childbirth, Antonio happily thinks of the stolen jewels; and, hoping to make the snooping Bosola believe he is casting a horoscope for the recovery of the stolen property, remarks:

> I have bin setting a figure
> For the Duchess Jewells.
>                     (II.ii.27–28)

Bosola, apparently knowing well the procedures by which such horoscopes are cast, asks:

> Ah: and how falls your question?
> Do you find it radicall?
>                     (II.ii.29–30)

Webster and other dramatists in this regard are utilizing the department of astrology known as *interrogations*—hence Bosola's query "how falls your question?" By means of this branch of the science, the astrologer could observe the configuration of the stars at the moment one asks him a question and thereby answer virtually any question imaginable: whether one absent be dead or alive, whether an unborn child shall be male or female, whether a man shall marry, whether a damsel be virtuous or a wife be with child, whether a voyage shall be successful, whether property lost shall be found, and so on.[1] The books of both Claudius Dariot and William Lilly, notable sixteenth and seventeenth century astrologers, are largely concerned with expounding astrological *interrogations,* and Lilly emphasizes especially questions concerning thefts and hidden property.[2]

In prognosticating for any interrogation, the astrologer must first determine whether or not the horoscope cast at the moment is *radical;*

---

[1] Cf. *infra,* pp. 119, 127.

[2] Claudius Dariot, *A Briefe and most easie Introduction to the Astrologicall Judgement of the Starres,* trans. Fabian Withers (London, 1598); and William Lilly, *Christian Astrology* (London, 1647, 1939).

that is, whether it generally corresponds to the questioner's *natal* horoscope.[3] For a horoscope cast to determine an interrogation can rightly
signify nothing unless it corresponds approximately to the horoscope
at birth. If, for instance, the natal horoscope shows that one shall be
unfortunate in his travels, it would be useless to seek from a later
horoscope an auspicious time for a journey—for in such case *all* times
would be unfortunate for travel. Bosola's query about the horoscope's
being *radical* is a rational and authenticated one, and shows Webster
to be not only well acquainted with the fact that horoscopes are cast for
discovering stolen goods and apprehending thieves but also well informed enough to know that such horoscopes must be *radical*.

Having first determined that the horoscope cast at the moment of
question is *radical,* the astrologer then observes the *significators*. The
significator of the questioner himself is the planet which rules the ascendant (the first house of the horoscope).[4] The significator of the
question is the planet which rules one of the other eleven houses of the
horoscope; that is, the significator regarding marital questions is usually the planet ruling the sign in the seventh house (the house of marriage); the significator concerning questions of journeys and voyages
is usually the planet ruling the sign in the ninth house (the house of
travel); and so on.[5]

Let us follow the astrologer as he attempts to determine the thief
and the location of some object that has been stolen. In most cases, the
ascendant signifies the place from where the goods were stolen; the
planet ruling the ascendant signifies the person who has been robbed;
the Moon and the planet ruling the second house signify the object
stolen; the fourth house and the planet ruling it signify the place where
the stolen goods are hidden; the seventh house and the planet ruling it
signify the thief.[6] In most cases also, the object shall be found if Luna
is approaching any one of three planets: (1) that ruling the ascendant,
(2) that ruling the twelfth house, (3) that ruling the house wherein is
posited the Moon. Otherwise it shall not be found—unless Luna is in

---

[3] Specifically, whether the *roots* (*radices*) or fundamental principles of the
two horoscopes are the same. See Lilly, *op. cit.,* pp. 74–75.

[4] If, for example, Aries is ascending, then Mars, being lord of Aries, signifies
the questioner.

[5] Cf. Lilly, pp. 75–77.

[6] *Ibid.,* pp. 207–208. I say "in most cases" because there are times when these
basic rules should be modified.

the ascendant or in the second house.[7] There is much more complexity
in the procedures, however, than these basic rules indicate; for Lilly
gives numerous instructions like the following:

If Luna be in the same quarter of the horoscope as the lord of the ascendant, and there is less than 30° between them, the thing lost is in or about the
owner's house; if there be more than 30° and less than 70° between them, it
is in the town where the owner resides; if they be not in the same quarter,
the owner is far from his stolen merchandize.[8]

By a glance at the horoscope and the planet signifying the thief, the
astute astrologer could cite many particulars regarding the culprit. The
planet signifying the thief indicates whether he were male or female,
young or old or middle-aged; and other celestial conditions informed
of the thief's exact age, the color of his clothes, whether one thief or
two, whether he stole maliciously or in jest, whether he is well-known
to the questioner, is a neighbor or kinsman, and so on.[9] Mercury as a
significator, for example, would suggest a culprit of

middling complexion; darkish hair; long face; high forehead; black or grey
eyes; thin beard or whiskers, often hardly any; slender, small legs; one
quick in walking, and full of talk and business.[10]

If the significator of the thief be in the last degrees of a sign, he is
"going off or leaving his lodgings"; if in an angle of the horoscope, he
is "still in town." If Saturn aspect the sign the Moon is in, the door of
the thief's house is "old and often in need of repair." If the planet ruling the seventh house be in the ascendant or if the Moon be in the
seventh house and approaching an aspect with Mars, Sol, or Mercury,
the thief will not be apprehended—provided his significator is fortunately aspected by Jupiter or Venus.[11]

This sixteenth-century Pinkerton could tell you just where the
stolen goods are hidden (in upper rooms or lower rooms, in a dairy or
washhouse, near a bridge or a gate or animals, in woods or bushes, behind a chimney or near a threshold, etc.), and which direction of the
compass one should take to recover them. He could tell you whether
the object stolen is heavy or light, what kind of commodity it is (such
as honey, fruit, silk, men's clothes, firearms); whether such goods will
be recovered, how many days or weeks or months it will take to recover them, and even whether the owner shall have to pay ransom.[12]

[7] *Ibid.*, pp. 134–136, 202, 207.     [8] *Ibid.*, p. 203.     [9] *Ibid.*, pp. 208–210.
[10] *Ibid.*, p. 218.     [11] *Ibid.*, pp. 211–219.     [12] *Ibid.*, pp. 214–217, 134–136.

By observing from what planet the planet ruling the ascendant last separated, he could tell how the object was lost.[13] If this planet separated last from Saturn, the object was lost through forgetfulness of the owner; if from Jupiter, through placing too much trust in the person by whom it was taken away; if from Venus, through such activities as drinking, gambling, making merry in a tavern, singing or dallying with women.[14]

In order to observe precisely how an astrologer used such information to "catch a thief" or locate stolen property, we may look at a horoscope in William Lilly's *Christian Astrology* (pp. 238–239) about which Lilly judged concerning the theft of money.

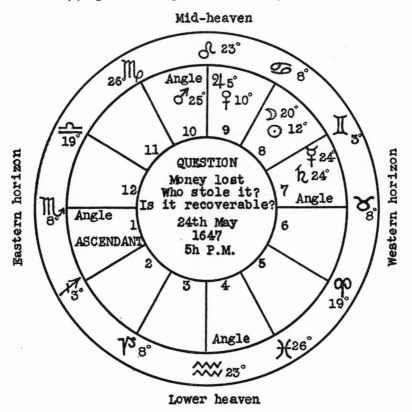

Mid-heaven

Eastern horizon

Western horizon

Lower heaven

---

[13] A planet is said to be *separating* from another when it is leaving an aspect with that planet. Cf. Lilly, p. 344.

[14] *Ibid.*, p. 203.

## LILLY'S JUDGMENT UPON THE ABOVE FIGURE

Here Scorpio ascends, and partly describes the questioner's person; Mars, lord of the ascendant, shows his mind and disposition. . . . Finding Mercury in an angle, having no essential dignities, and in partile conjunction of Saturn, and square of Mars, I took him to signify the thief. But whether he described a male or female was the question. The Moon was in a masculine sign, applying to a masculine planet (Mars), and Mercury was in conjunction with Saturn, and square to Mars, both masculine planets; I judged, therefore, that the sex was male.

As Mercury ever signified youth, . . . I said he was a youth, of some 15 or 16. I described him of reasonable stature, thin visaged, hanging eyebrows, with some scar or blemish in his face, because Mars cast his square to Mercury; bad eyesight, as Mercury is with evil fixed stars (the Pleiades) of the nature of Mars and Luna; dark hair, because of his closeness to Saturn; a scurvy countenance, and one formerly accused of theft and knavery.

The youth's significator being in conjunction with Saturn, lord of the third and fourth houses, I judged him the child of some neighbor; and as Luna is in Gemini, and Mercury in Taurus in the seventh house, I said he dwelt either opposite the questioner, or a little south-west. . . . As Luna applied to sextile with Mars, lord of the ascendant, and was within about four degrees of the aspect, I judged he should . . . have his money again within four days. . . . The event proved me right, both as to the person and the return of the money, which was within three days after.

In this fashion, therefore, did the astrologer work when he desired to relieve his client's mind regarding an absconded servant, stolen money, or any other similar mishap which might occur in the daily routine of his affairs; and such is the kind of astrology to which Webster, Wilson, and other Jacobean dramatists occasionally referred.

## CHAPTER TWELVE

# NON-ALCHEMICAL PSEUDO-SCIENCES
## IN *The Alchemist*

SUBTLE, the ringleader of the tricksters in Ben Jonson's *The Alchemist,* occasionally cozened his clients with pseudo-scientific lore other than alchemical. An analysis of Subtle's remarks on physiognomy, chiromancy, metoposcopy, and astrology in the light of contemporary texts on these pseudo-sciences reveals that Subtle was usually (but not always) technically accurate when he threw together impressively various bits of pseudo-scientific lore.

Abel Drugger—the second dupe whom Subtle's procurer, Face, brings into the snares of the tricksters—eagerly expects to learn how to be successful in his tobacco business and avowedly wishes that the door of his newly-erected shop be constructed by the laws of necromancy.[1] Immediately Subtle pronounces unctuously that Drugger is "a fortunate fellow" and "in right way to'ward riches";[2] and when Face cunningly asks in pretended amazement how so much fortune can be remarked so soon, Subtle retorts knowingly:

> By a rule, Captaine,
> In *metoposcopie,* which I doe worke by,
> A certaine starre i'the fore-head, which you see not.
> Your chest-nut, or your olive-colour'd face
> Do's never faile: and your long eare doth promise.
> I knew't, by certaine spots too, in his teeth,
> And on the naile of his *mercurial* finger.
> *Face:* Which finger's that?
> *Subtle:* His little finger. Looke.
> Yo'were borne upon a wensday?
> *Drugger:* Yes, indeed, sir.
> *Subtle:* The thumbe, in *chiromantie,* we give VENUS;

[1] I.iii.11 (Herford and Simpson edition).
[2] I.iii.33-35.

The forefinger to JOVE; the midst, to SATURNE:
The ring to SOL; the least, to MERCURIE:
Who was the lord, sir of his *horoscope,*
His *house of life* being *Libra,* which fore-shew'd
He should be a merchant, and should trade with ballance.[3]

In this fashion Subtle persuades his client that he is proficient in metoposcopy, physiognomy, chiromancy, and astrology.

Subtle's remarks are considerably clearer when compared with the
accounts in Richard Saunders' large tome, wherein are recorded metic-
ulously the tenets of these pseudo-sciences. Says he:

Now . . . in . . . Metoposcopy, we must treat of the lines of the forehead
and their significations, and . . . of the Characters of the Planets, . . . A
Planetary line is that which is referred to some of the Planets, which are
placed on the forehead, . . . The first line is that of *Saturn,* appears neer
the hair; that which is under it is *Jupiter's,* the third belongs to *Mars,* the
other four are in the superficies of the forehead, as the *Sun* and *Moon* upon
the eyes, *Mercury* neer the grissell of the nose, *Venus* above it between the
eyes. . . . In these lines are the infallible signs of the temperaments, and of
man's life, . . . If the line of *Jupiter* be longer then that of *Saturn,* it denotes riches. . . . A line broken or discontinued . . . denotes misfortunes
in War. . . . The *Moon* line being clear, distinct and perfect above the left
eye, signifies much travel into strange Nations, . . .[4]

The colours of the Body, and especially of the face, denote the Humour
and inclination of the person; . . . A green colour that is obscure and
black, speaks a Cholerick person; those who are ruddy and red, and are
lean withal, are neat, cunning, and subtile; . . . Those that be chestnut
or olive colour are Jovialists and honest people, open without painting or
cheating; . . .[5]

Those that have ears somewhat long, are bold, impudent, unlearned,
gluttons, and whoremaster.[6]

When we would draw any judgment from the nayls we are to observe
these things, viz. Whether they are broad, white, narrow, long, oblique,
little, round, fleshy, pale, black, yellowish, red, and *marked.* . . . Marked

[3] I.iii.43–57. There are virtually no annotations on these lines in any of the
various editions of *The Alchemist.*

[4] *Physiognomie, and Chiromancie, Metoposcopie, Dreams, and the Art of
Memory* (London, 1653), pp. 163–164.

[5] *Ibid.,* pp. 166–167.

[6] *Ibid.,* p. 176. Cf, however, Arcandam's statement: "When Eares be great and
hang downward, they signifie riches." *The Most Excellent . . . Booke of . . .
Arcandam, . . . With an Addition of Physiognomie* (London, 1634), sig. L4v.
This text appeared frequently between 1562 and 1637.

Nails signifie a Cholerick and Martial Nature, given to cruelty; and as many little marks as there are, they speak so many evil desires, . . .[7]

When thou wouldst know the nativity of some one, take the hand wherein thou findest the Lines are most fair, clear, and distinct; above all . . . consider the middle natural Line, where it ends; . . . for if the Line ends towards the mount of Mercury, the party is born on a Wednesday, in the months of May or August.[8]

You are then to note, that the thumb . . . is dedicated to *Venus;* . . . the Indix finger . . . is attributed to *Jupiter.* The third, called the middle finger, . . . is *Saturnus.* . . . As for the Ring-finger, this is dedicated to the *Sun.* . . . The last and least . . . is attributed to Mercury. . . . In these verses you have a short learned description:

> Venus *the Thumb,* Jove *in the Index joyes,*
> Saturn *the Middle,* Sol *the youthful toyes:*
> Stilborn *the Least,* Luna *the Ferients,*
> *In Cavea* Mars *delights to pitch his Tents.*[9]

Thus Subtle's remarks on metoposcopy, physiognomy, and chiromancy have a sound basis in the pseudo-scientific texts of the time.

Subtle's astrology, on the other hand, is partly correct and partly not. Anyone familiar with the manifestations of an astrologer knows that Subtle possessed neither time nor information sufficient to cast Drugger's horoscope—to identify the planet Mercury as the "lord of the horoscope" and Libra as the zodiacal sign governing the horoscope's "house of life." Apparently it is because Drugger makes known immediately upon his arrival his wish to have his economic activities free from such things as a bankruptcy that the planet Mercury is quickly and appropriately brought to sly Subtle's mind. For even a gull—and

---

[7] Saunders, *op. cit.,* pp. 69, 74. In Geronimo Cortes' *Phisonomia* (Cordova, 1601; Tarragona, 1609), fols. 107v–112r, we find that "a white spot in the middle of the thumb nail denotes some undertaking or important business of great profit, while a black spot there indicates expenditure and loss of money." Cited by Lynn Thorndike, *A History of Magic and Experimental Science* (New York, 1941), vi, 168.

[8] Saunders, p. 26.

[9] *Ibid.,* pp. 11–12. Saunders' prose in this passage is found also in Rudolphus Goclenius, *Uranoscopia chiroscopia et metoposcopia* (Francofurti, 1608), p. 176; and the verse is found in both Latin and English in *The Art of Divining,* Englished by George Wharton (London, 1652), p. 4, a translation of Johann Rothmann's *Chiromantiae* . . . (Erfurt, 1595). Apparently this verse, which Jonson is obviously reproducing, was a commonplace comparable to "Thirty days hath September, . . ."

certainly the audience—knew that the planet Mercury ruled over all things pertaining to business. Claudius Ptolemy, astrology's most authoritative spokesman, writes: "Mercury produces superintendents of business, accountants, . . . merchants and bankers, . . . and in short all who live by . . . stipend, salary, or allowance." [10] Claudius Dariotus says that Mercury governs ". . . arithmeticians, marchants, ingenious workmen in everye thinge, . . . industry, honest labor, . . . and of the sayd thinges it yeildeth riches." [11] Augier Ferrier writes that Mercury rules "Notaries, Registrars, . . . Mathematicians, Messengers, and traders. . . . Merchants and busiefellowes." [12] And William Lilly reports: "Mercury generally signifies . . . merchants, . . . exchangers of money, clerks, . . . accomptants, . . . busy secretaries, . . ." [13] Moreover, Libra was that sign of the zodiac which was represented even in the common almanacks by the Scales or the Balance. Therefore Libra was likewise brought to Subtle's cozening mind.

But, according to all astrologers, Libra cannot govern the "house of life" if Mercury is "lord of the horoscope." The sign of the zodiac ascending on the eastern horizon at one's birth governed what was called the "first house" of the horoscope; and since it was from this house that the astrologers gained "signification of the *life* of man, of his stature, colour, complexion, form, and shape," it was known as the *House of Life*. [14] Each sign of the zodiac was ruled by a particular planet; and that planet which ruled the sign which happened to be in the *House of Life*—and was therefore considered the planet which influenced most the affairs of the person—was called the *Lord of the Horoscope*. [15] Thus if Libra governed the *House of Life*, then Venus (who ruled Libra) must have been the *Lord of the Horoscope*. But inasmuch as Subtle wanted Drugger's horoscope conducive to riches and fortune in business, he selected appropriately (for his cozening pur-

---

[10] *Tetrabiblos or Quadripartite,* trans. J. M. Ashmand (London, 1822; Chicago, 1936), Bk. IV, ch. iv.

[11] *A Briefe and most easie Introduction to the Astrologicall Judgement of the Starres* (London, 1598), sig. D4r.

[12] *A Learned Astronomical Discourse of the Judgement of Nativities* (London, 1593), pp. 26, 32.

[13] *Christian Astrology* (London, 1647), edited (as *An Introduction to Astrology by William Lilly*) by Zadkiel (London, 1852; 1939), p. 49.

[14] *Ibid.,* p. 28.

[15] *Ibid.,* pp. 343, 61–62.

poses) the planet Mercury and the sign of Libra. He doubtless realized also that a horoscope governed by Mercury with Libra ascending was a breach of technicalities that his gull Drugger would completely overlook.

No books on astrology, physiognomy, chiromancy, or metoposcopy that are definitely from Jonson's library have been traced.[16] There existed many, however, which Jonson could have used.[17] At the beginning of his epitome, Richard Saunders cites a bibliography of nearly two hundred authors whose works he has drawn upon. Inasmuch as the writers on these sciences invariably drew largely upon previous works, copied predecessors oftentimes verbatim, it is highly improbable that any particular text can be cited as Jonson's immediate source. But it is evident that he was familiar with some of these tomes of arcana, and that Subtle in utilizing this material was but dallying with the gulls brought before him.[18]

[16] Cf. C. H. Herford and Percy Simpson, "Books in Jonson's Library," in *Ben Jonson* (Oxford, 1925), I, 250–271.

[17] In addition to texts already mentioned, cf. *Chyromantie ac physionomie Anastasis* of Cocles, *Introductiones apotelesmaticae . . . in chyromantiam physiognomiam astrologiam naturalem . . .* of Johann ab Indagine, *Aphorismorum Metoposcopicorum libellus unus* of Thaddaeus Hagecius, and *De humana physiognomia* of Giovanni Battista Porta. The numerous editions of each of these bespeak their wide dissemination throughout the sixteenth century. Both Cocles and Indagine enjoyed English translations.

[18] The materials in this chapter appeared first in *PQ*, XXIV (1945), 85–89. For making available certain rare books used herein I express gratitude to the University of Alabama Research Committee.

# Sources of the Renaissance Englishman's Knowledge of Astrology

*A Bibliographical Survey and a Bibliography*

## I

Astrology originated somewhere in the Chaldean East, spread to Egypt, and thence to the ancient world of Greece. Eventually passing to the Roman Empire, accounts of the influences of the signs and planets by various Chaldeans, Egyptians, Greeks, and Romans were augmented, synthesized, and preserved by astrologers, poets, physicians, and scientists who had a flair for writing.[1] One of the earliest of these works preserved for posterity is the *Astronomicon,* a lengthy poem composed in the first century A.D. by the Roman poet Marcus Manilius.[2] In the second century, the great astronomer and mathematician, Claudius Ptolemy, produced a work entitled *Tetrabiblos or Quadripartitum,* or *Four Books on the Influence of the Stars;* and, perhaps because of his authorship of the *Almagest* which handed to posterity the Ptolemaic system of the universe, his text on astrology remained a leading authoritative work in the field for more than fifteen centuries. Appearing in the same period were the earliest texts we have associating astrology with medicine: *De diebus decretoriis (The Critical Days)* and *Prognostica de decubitu infirmorum (The Prognostication of Disease)* by the great physician Galen, and the *Iatromathematica (Predicting Illness by the Stars)* of Hermes Trismegistus. In the fourth century, Julius Firmicus

---

[1] Cf. T. O. Wedel, *The Mediaeval Attitude Toward Astrology* (Yale University Press, 1919), pp. 1–24; Lynn Thorndike, *A History of Magic and Experimental Science* (New York, 1923), II, 13–35; A. E. Thierens, *Astrology in Mesopotamian Culture* (Leiden, 1935); C. V. McLean, *Babylonian Astrology and Its Relation to the Old Testament* (Toronto, 1929); and A. Bouche-Leclercq, *L'Astrologie Grecque* (Paris, 1899).

[2] Many editions of this work appeared in the fifteenth and sixteenth centuries (see Bibliography). See also *The Five Books of M. Manilius, containing a system of the ancient astronomy and astrology: . . . Done into English verse from the Latin, with Notes* (London, 1697); or the more modern English edition prepared by A. E. Housman.

Maternus compiled a text of genethliacal astrology entitled *Matheseos,* the longest and most elaborate of the extant treatises on the subject of natal horoscopes.[3]

Astrology preserved its place in the intellectual milieu of the Western World through Mohammedan channels. The early Church Fathers condemned it as "a diabolical manifestation of pagan impiety," but the science spread from the Moslem world to the Saracen schools at Toledo and Cordova, where in the twelfth century the texts of the Arabian-Jewish astrologers were studied and—along with Ptolemy's *Tetrabiblos*—translated into Latin by Western scholars.[4] At these Spanish centers of scientific learning were promulgated the works of the celebrated Arabian astrologer, Albumasar, whose two principal books were entitled *Liber introductorius major* (*The Greater Introduction to Astronomy*) and *De magnis conjunctionibus* (*The Book of Great Conjunctions*).[5] Another important Arabian astrologer was Alchabitius, whose principal work was his *Libellus isagogicus judicorum astrorum* (*Introduction to Judicial Astrology*).[6] The most complete of the Arabic works on astrology was that of Albohazen Haly filius Abenragel entitled *Liber completus in judiciis astorum* (*The Complete Book of Judicial Astrology*).[7] Perhaps the most outstanding Jewish astrologer was Abraham ibn Ezra, whose principal published work was his *Liber de*

[3] For Galen and Hermes, see Thorndike, *op. cit.,* i, 178 ff., 287 ff. The works of Ptolemy and Maternus are discussed more fully anon.

[4] Cf. Charles H. Haskins, *Studies in Mediaeval Science* (New York, 1927); Pierre Duhem, *Le Systeme du Monde* (Paris, 1915–17); George Sarton, *An Introduction to the History of Science* (Baltimore, 1927–31); and Thorndike, *op. cit.,* i, 691–697; 710 ff.

[5] This is Abu Ma'shar Ja'far ibn Muhammad ibn 'Umar al-Balkhi, who flourished in Bagdad and died in 886. Both of these works were translated in the twelfth century by John of Spain (or Seville), were first published at Augsburg in 1489 and enjoyed considerable reputation thereafter. Cf. Sarton, i, 568; Thorndike, i, 649–651; Duhem, iii, 174–176, 369–386. J. C. Houzeau and A. Lancaster, *Bibliographie generale de l'astronomie* (Brussels, 1887), i, 702–705, list about thirty different tracts by Albumasar existant in manuscript form.

[6] This is Abu-l-Saqr 'Abd al-'Aziz ibn 'Uthman ibn 'Ali al-Qabisi, who lived in the tenth century and whose works were translated in the twelfth by John of Spain. John's translation, *Alchabitii Abdilazi liber introductorius ad magisterium judiciorum,* was printed innumerable times. See Bibliography and Sarton, i, 669.

[7] This is Abu-l-Hazen 'Ali ibn abi-l-Rijal al-Saibani al-Katib al-Maghribi. Abenragel was his father's name rather than his own; hence the appellation Albohazen Haly *filius* Abenragel. He flourished at a period when Arabian astrology was fully developed. His work was translated in the thirteenth century and printed many times: in 1485, 1503, 1551, 1571, etc. He is not to be confused with Albohali, who wrote *Albohali Arabis astrologi antiquissimi . . . de judiciis nativitatum liber,* published at Nuremburg, 1546.

*nativitatibus* (*The Book of Nativities*).[8] Notable names of other Arabian and Jewish astrologers include Alkindi, Thebit ben Corat, Rhazes (Rasis), Messahala, Albohali, Omar ben Alphorkham, Abubekr, Almansor, Zael, and others.[9] In the mediaeval centuries following them their works were augmented and disseminated by the manuscript treatises of such eminent professional adepts as Michael Scot, Guido Bonatus, and John Ganivet.[10]

Although astrological learning apparently centered in Spain, Italy, and France in the late mediaeval centuries, England shared also in the diffusion of Arabic science and astrology in Western Europe—many Englishmen being translators or writers of astrological treatises.[11] Richard of Wallingford (1292–1336), a member of the Oxford faculty and later Abbot of St. Albans, wrote an astrological textbook entitled *De judiciis astronomicis*.[12] His contemporary, William Grizannte, wrote a *Speculum astrologiae* and a *De qualitatibus astrorum*.[13] John Eschendon (Eschuid?), another member of the Oxford faculty in the fourteenth century, wrote an elaborate textbook entitled *Summa astrologiae*.[14] Still another Oxford professor, Simon Bredon, in his will dated 1368, bequeathed to several colleges his extensive scientific library; and, more important now, he listed his books. In the catalogue of the library of this prominent fourteenth-century man-of-science are listed the works of Ptolemy, Albumasar, Haly Abenragel, and others.[15] Indeed, astrology is more voluminously represented in his library than is any other science. It is no wonder that Chaucer wrote that "hende Nicholas," Oxford scholar,

> Hadde lerned art, but al his fantasye
> Was turned for to lerne astrologye.
> (*C.T.*, A, 3191–92)

In the last two decades of the fifteenth century and the first half of the sixteenth century, the advent of the printing press brought the publication

---

[8] Cf. *The Beginning of Wisdom, An Astrological Treatise by Abraham ibn Ezra,* edited by Raphael Levy and Francisco Cantera (Baltimore, 1939), esp. pp. 13–14.

[9] Cf. Thorndike, I, 641 ff., II, 66 ff. The prominent Latin translators of these Arabic and Jewish works were John of Spain (or Seville), Plato of Tivoli, Robert of Chester, Herman of Dalmatia, Hugh of Santalia, Gerard of Cremona, and Peter of Abano.

[10] See Haskins, 242–298; Thorndike, II, 307–337, 825–840.

[11] See Haskins' chapter, "The Introduction of Arabic Science into England," *op. cit.,* pp. 113–139; Thorndike's chapter "Some Twelfth Century Translators of Astrology from the Arabic," *op. cit.,* II, 66–98, as well as II, 171–187.

[12] R. T. Gunther, *Early Science in Oxford* (Oxford, 1923), II, 48–50. Cf. also Thorndike, III, 119 ff.

[13] Gunther, II, 44.

[14] Cf. Thorndike, III, 325 ff., 717 ff.

[15] Gunther, II, 52–55.

and re-publication of a host of these important mediaeval astrological texts as well as new treatises by fifteenth and sixteenth century writers. From the Continental publishing meccas came numerous editions of the works of Ptolemy, Hermes Trismegistus, Firmicus Maternus, Alchabitius, Abraham ibn Ezra, Albohazen Haly, Albumasar, and Guido Bonatus. There were many others.[16]

Since the astrological treatises of the mediaeval "authorities" were frequently the "best sellers" of the incunabula period, they were consequently familiar works to all well-read people of the early sixteenth century.[17] Among the books given to Oxford University in 1439–1444 by the early patron of Renaissance learning, Duke Humphrey of Gloucester, were works of astrology by Haly Abenragel, Rhazes, Zael, Albumasar, Ptolemy, Thebit ben Corat, Eschendon, and Bonatus.[18] The famous collections of books brought to England by John Tiptoft and other Humanists after their Continental travels must have contained similar items. In 1520 Thomas Linacre compiled a list of the books owned by William Grocyn, one of the patriarchs of Humanistic learning in England; and on this list are Marcus Manilius' *Astronomicon,* Ptolemy's *Quadripartitum,* Bethem's *Centiloquium* and *De horis planetariis,* and two copies of Alchabitius' *Liber isogogicus.*[19] In the Oxford bookseller John Dorne's *Day Book,* a ledger in which Dorne noted each day the names of all the books he sold during the year 1520, are listed a copy of Abraham ibn Ezra's *De nativitatibus,* a "ptholomaeus 2 quarterni," and eighty-one Prognostications (28 in Latin and 53 "in englis").[20] In the list of books and manuscripts belonging a generation later to Dr. John Dee (1554–1607) is this astounding list of pertinent titles:

*Ptolomaei quadripartitum* (Lat.)
*Commentum super Centiloquium Ptolomaei*
*Liber florum Albumasar* (2 copies)
*Liber experimentorum Albumasar*

[16] See Bibliography.

[17] Cf. Thorndike, iv, chs. lxi–lxiv; and also George Sarton, "The Scientific Literature Transmitted through the Incunabula," *Osiris,* v (1938), 42–245.

[18] Lists are in Henry Anstey, *Munimenta Academica* (London, 1868), ii, 758–772, and in his *Epistolae Academiae Oxon* (Oxford, 1898), pp. 179–184, 232–237.

[19] Montague Burrows, ed., *Collectanea, Second Series,* Oxford Historical Society (Oxford, 1890), pp. 317–331 (esp. pp. 323, 329).

[20] Falconer Madan, ed., *Collectanea, First Series,* Oxford Historical Society (Oxford, 1885), pp. 71–177; and Burrows, *op. cit.,* pp. 452 ff. Other significant items in Dorne's ledger are *practica rasis* (2 copies), *liber Xii prophetarum, Egidius de urinarum judiciis* (2 copies), *stella clericorum* (2 copies), *Summa godfredi,* and *Petrus de ayliaco de ymagine mundi.* A more thorough investigation and analysis of the works in this *Day Book* would undoubtedly prove interesting and informing.

*Albumasar introductorium*
*Albumasar de judiciis astrologicis*
*Albumasar de revolutionibus*
*Summae excerptae ex libro Albumasar, de revolutione nativitatum*
*Haly de judiciis astrorum* (2 copies)
*Albohali de nativitatibus*
*Alcabicius, Astronomia quaedam judicialis*
*Alcabicii astrologia*
*Messahala de nativitatibus*
*Jacob Alkindus de judiciis astrologicis*
*Jacobi Alkindi liber de aspectibus*
*Zahelis introductorium, cum judiciis sequentibus*
*Abraham Judaei liber de judiciis nativitatum*
*Zaelis electiones*
*Guido Bonatus de judiciis astrorum*
*Guido Bonatus de astrologio*
*Liber novem judicum in astrologia*
*Introductiones astronomicae*
*Hermetis liber de septem planetis*
*Mathematica Alexandri summi astrologi*
*Aristotelis commentum in astrologiam*
*Astronomica, astrologica, et arithmetica*
*De significatione planetarum, cum aliis tractatibus*
*Libri diversi astrologici*
*Hippocratis astronomia de infirmitatibus*
*Hippocratis prognostica*[21]

The library of the learned Sir Thomas Smith, Cambridge professor and (according to Willard Farnham) "a man of solid substance and wide experience in public service," contained in 1566 the following:

*Cardanus super Quadripartitum Ptolomaei*
*Johann Pontani in Quadripart. Ptolomaei*
*Firmicus Maternus*
*Haly de Judiciis*
*Abrah. Judaeus, de Nativitate, & ix Judicum*
*Elcabitius, &c.*
*Guido Bonatus*
*Lucas Gauricus*
*Schonerus de Nativitatibus*
*Cyprianus Leovitius*
*Appianus & Astronomia Gebri*
*Cornel. Agrippa de occult Philosoph.*
*De Praedictione Astronom.*

[21] *The Private Diary of Dr. John Dee, and the Catalogue of his Library of Manuscripts,* ed., J. P. Halliwell-Phillipps, Camden Society Publications (London, 1842), pp. 65–98. Cf. also Montague R. James, *Lists of Manuscripts Formerly Owned by Dr. John Dee* (Oxford, 1921).

*Ephemerides Simi Cardani, de Judiciis, &c.*
[Numerous copies of *Galen*] [22]

Many Elizabethan writers mention standard authors in the field of astrology as if the former were well acquainted with the latter's works.[23] In his *Astrologaster* (London, 1620), Thomas Melton mentions Messahala, Abenragel, Alchabitius, Albumasar, Abraham Avenezra (ibn Ezra), Hermes Trismegistus, Thebit ben Corat, Firmicus Maternus, Abraham Haly, Erra Pater, and Durbachius.[24] In William Lilly's elaborate textbook, *Christian Astrology* (London, 1647), the author lists a bibliography of more than a dozen pages (including one hundred and ninety-five titles) and states that he possesses every book he lists.

## II

Probably the most widely disseminated and admittedly authoritative astrology textbook of the fifteenth and sixteenth centuries was Claudius Ptolemy's *Tetrabiblos* or *Quadripartitum,* although it did not by any means contain all the elements or technicalities of the science.[25] Ptolemy begins

[22] John Strype, *Life of the Learned Sir Thomas Smith* (London, 1698), pp. 139–147.

[23] Cf. Richard Harvey, *Astrological Discourse* (1583), Leonard Digges, *A Prognostication of right good effect* (1585); Thomas Nashe, *A Wonderful Prognostication* (1591); Sir Christopher Heydon, *Defense of Judicial Astrologie* (1603).

[24] Page 12, *et passim.*

[25] The *Quadripartitum* was preserved when the Arabian scientists in the ninth century translated all of Ptolemy's works into Arabic. These collected works passed to the European world under their Arabic title *Almagest,* a Latin translation of which was made in 1175 at Toledo by the renown translator Gerard of Cremona.
The first publication of the *Quadripartitum* was a Latin version (from the Arabic) at Venice in 1484, reprinted in 1493 and 1519. Joachimo Camerario's Latin version was printed at Basle in 1533 (in the edition of Firmicus Maternus' *Astronomicon libri viii*); reprinted in 1551. Camerario's version, accompanied by a Greek text, appeared also at Nuremburg in 1535, and again at Basle in 1540 and 1541. Philip Melanchthon's translation (also with Greek text) was issued at Basle in 1553 and at Prague in 1610. Jerome Cardan's translation (Latin version only) appeared at Basle in 1554, 1555, 1559, 1568, 1576, 1579?, and 1583. Antony Gogava's Latin translation appeared at Louvain in 1548. Francis Junctin's edition (with Greek text and enormous commentaries) appeared at Lyons in 1581 and 1583.
The first English translation was published in London in 1701, by John Whalley. A second edition of Whalley's translation was issued in 1768. A better translation (based on Proclus' Greek text) was published in London by J. M.

his book with a discussion of the validity of astrology, and after this pre-
liminary defense devotes the remainder of the first book to a discussion of
the elemental qualities of the planets and a delineation of the basic terms
of the science. The second book is devoted to the prediction of general or
universal events, or those which concern entire nations or large territories
and communities—predictions of war, pestilence, famine, drought, innundations, and similar visitations. Such predictions (according to Ptolemy) are
determined by the eclipses of the sun and moon and the positions of the
planets during the eclipse. The last two books of the *Quadripartitum* deal
with the prediction of particular events in the lives of individuals. In these
books Ptolemy discusses conception and birth, predictions concerning parents, brothers and sisters, sex, twins, monstrous births, length of life, shape
and temperament of the body, injuries and diseases of the body, quality and
diseases of the mind, as well as the individual's wealth, profession and employment, marriage, children, friends and enemies, travels, periodic divisions of life, and the nature of the individual's death.

An even more comprehensive textbook of antique genethliacal astrology
was the *De nativitatibus* or *Matheseos libri viii* of Julius Firmicus Maternus.[26] Like Ptolemy, Maternus devotes his first book to an attack on those
who accuse astrologers of being irreligious and of pretending to be infallible. His second book discusses the basic principles and terms of the science
and the elemental qualities of the planets. But the remaining six books give
information for a complete delineation of the natal horoscope. Book III
deals principally with the significance of each planet (and combinations of
planets) in each of the twelve houses of the horoscope. Book IV informs
chiefly about the influence of the Moon when she is aspected by each of the
other planets. Book V interprets the meaning of each sign and each planet
in each house of the horoscope, and of each planet when posited in each of
the twelve signs of the zodiac. Book VI gives a detailed account of the
various aspects between planets, and discusses numerous complex planetary

---

Ashmand in 1822 (reprinted by the Aries Press, Chicago, 1936). The edition for
the Loeb Classical Library was issued in 1941 by Frank E. Robbins.

Ptolemy's *Centiloquium,* a list of one hundred astrological aphorisms, was also
printed innumerable times, frequently at the end of the *Quadripartitum.* A
*Centiloquium* or *Aphorismi* was composed also by Bethem, Almansor, and
Hermes (all reprinted in Firmicus Maternus' *Astronomicon Libri VIII,* Basle,
1551, and in Francis Junctin's *Speculum Astrologiae,* Lyons, 1581, 1583).

[26] A partial edition of Books III–V of the *Matheseos* was published at Venice
in 1488 and 1494 (in *Opus astrolabii plani . . . a Johanne Anglie*). The complete *Matheseos libri viii* was first published at Venice in 1497. An Aldine edition
was issued in 1499 and 1503 (entitled *Astronomicorum libri octo*). Editions by
Nicholas Pruckner, which reproduced the Aldine text, appeared at Basle in 1533
and 1551. See *Julii Firmici Materni Matheseos Libri VIII,* ed. W. Kroll and F.
Skutsch (Leipzig, 1879–1913). No translation has been made into English.

positions (such as Mercury and Venus and Mars all posited in the ninth house). Books VII and VIII discuss still further the many intricacies of the natal horoscope.

One of the most popular and complete mediaeval textbooks of astrology passed on to the sixteenth century was the *Liber astronomicus* of Guido Bonatus, eminent professional astrologer of the thirteenth century.[27] The *Liber astronomicus* is a voluminous work of ten books, in which Bonatus proposes to compile from past authorities a complete and understandable textbook of astrology. He employs the antique works of Ptolemy, Hermes Trismegistus, and Dorotheus, but chiefly the more modern treatises of such Arabian astrologers as Alchabitius, Albumasar, Messahala, Albohazen Haly, and Thebit ben Corat, as well as inserting in his compendium some additions of his own. His first book in the *Liber astronomicus* is a general introduction in which he defines his subject, discusses its utility, and meets objections of his opponents. The second book deals with the signs of the zodiac; the third book discusses the planets and their influences; the fourth treats chiefly of planetary conjunctions. The remaining six books are devoted to the subject of astrological judgments, and with the four chief departments of astrological prediction into which the science had evolved during the late mediaeval period (i.e., *interrogations, elections, revolutions,* and *nativities*). In his book on *nativities,* the department of astrology in which predictions are made for the individual on the basis of his natal horoscope, Guido discloses one's destiny regarding character, physical and mental qualities, maladies, travels, profession, marriage, friends, enemies, religion, length of life, as well as the fate of one's brothers, parents, children, serfs, and domestic animals. In his book on *interrogations,* Guido answers "questions" on all sorts of matters, such as the discovery of a thief or a lost article, the trustworthiness of a friend or ally, the status of a prospective marriage-partner, the kind of food to be served at a dinner to which one has been invited. In the book on *elections,* Guido tells how to select the propitious moment for undertaking (or electing) almost any act of daily life: the proper time for beginning a journey, writing a letter, paring the nails, trimming the beard, taking a bath. In the book on *revolutions,* he tells how —by means of planetary revolutions together with eclipses, comets, and conjunctions—the astrologer predicts for nations and large territorial areas regarding war, pestilence, floods, earthquakes, changes in political or religious institutions, the fate of monarchs, and even the prospects for a good crop of melons. The *Liber astronomicus* was perhaps the most thorough and elaborate treatise on astrology that the Renaissance inherited from the mediaeval period.

[27] The *Liber astronomicus* was first published at Augsburg in 1491. Other editions appeared at Venice in 1506, at Basle in 1530, 1550, and 1572, at Augsburg in 1581. Cf. Thorndike, ii, 826, 839.

The most complete and influential work on astrological medicine was John Ganivet's *Amicus medicorum (The Friend of Physicians)*.[28] The first of the four parts of this book establishes the orthodoxy of astrology in medical practice. The second division deals with the basic principles and terms of the science and with the general influences of the planets. The third division discusses the sources of pestilence and death, and how to prognosticate regarding these. The fourth division is concerned with astrological instructions for preserving health, expelling disease, and concocting medicinal cures; how to comfort each of the four humours of the body when a corresponding constellation reigns in the heavens, how to purge bad humours according to planetary aspects, how to cure fevers and innumerable diseases, how and when to perform phlebotomy or administer cordials.

These four works whose contents have been outlined somewhat extensively are texts from which one might glean expert astrological information. They are chiefly the source-books, so to speak, for the hundreds of other treatises published in the sixteenth century. Material in them was re-hashed again and again in the copious printings of the texts of such outstanding sixteenth-century astrologers as John Indagine, Luke Gauric, Augier Ferrier, Jerome Cardan, Claudius Dariot, John Taisnier, John Schoener, John Garcaeus, Antony Mizauld, Marsiglio Ficino, Henricus Rantzovius, Rudolph Goclenius, Caspar Peucer, and Francis Junctin. Astrology never developed beyond a composite system based on the materials of Ptolemy, Firmicus Maternus, and the principal Arabian astrologers. Francis Junctin's magnificent two-volume *Speculum astrologiae* (Lyons, 1573), the most elaborate compendium of astrology ever published, was compiled chiefly by citing the significant remarks of many past authorities on almost any aspect of astrology imaginable. Some of the horoscope-casters of a later day might have had more to say than had the mediaevalists, but there was little in their utterances that was significantly novel. All of them copied the "masters," and—one may add—each other.

### III

The knowledge of astrology possessed by the *average* sixteenth-century Englishman was probably not derived from the authoritative textbook of astrology (such as those we have been discussing), but rather from simple handbooks, prognostications, and astrological sections in popular encyclopedias of learning in the vernacular.[29] The *De proprietatibus rerum* of

[28] The *Amicus medicorum* was written in 1431, printed at Lyons in 1496, 1508, 1550, 1596, and at Frankfort in 1614. Surprisingly it is not found in the libraries of either Dee or Smith, though both possessed astrological works by Hippocrates and Galen.

[29] Cf. Louis B. Wright, *Middle-Class Culture in Elizabethan England* (Chapel Hill, 1935), *passim*, esp. ch. xv.

Bartholomaeus Anglicus was such an encyclopedia, designed for the average reader rather than for the scholar and expert.[30] The eighth book of this work is devoted to a discussion of the world, the heavens, the signs of the zodiac, the planets, the "Moon's Properties," the Dragon's Head and Tail, "the Starre Cometa." But Bartholomaeus has merely culled in the baldest fashion a hodge-podge of astrological matter from Albertus Magnus, Ptolemy, and the Arabian astrologers. He has filched and restated only the prominent characteristics of each planet and sign, has given no thought to informing his reader how to use this information or how to cast a horoscope.

One could find a somewhat better exposition of astrology than in the *De proprietatibus rerum* in the encyclopedic handbook known as *The Kalender of Shepherdes,* a translation of the French *Le Compost et Kalendrier des bergiers.*[31] The last of the five divisions of this work is devoted to "Astrology and Physiognomy." After discussing the nature of the heavens, the signs of the zodiac, the houses of the heavens through which the planets and signs continually pass, the association of the signs and planets, and so on, the author describes the "propryties" and influences of each planet—illustrated, for example, by the following for Mercury:

Next . . . is Mercury / he is ful drye of his nature / his two synes is Jeminy & Virgo / . . . . They that be borne under mercurys / be subtyle of wyt & shall be of good governaunce / for women he shall have blame / and he shall nat set by mariage he wyll love ladyes and he shulde be a gode man of the churche and relygious and be happy to marchandyse / he shall gader great gode and be crafty in reteryke phylosophy and gemetry / he shall love all maner instrumentys of musyke / and a clothemaker / he shall have a hye forhede longe face and a thyn berde and a great pleder / Under his governaunce is the flanke the thyes and the bely.[32]

Then in a section entitled "To knowe the fortunes and destinies of a man borne under the xii synges after Ptholomaeus prynce of astronomy," [33] the

[30] The first printed edition of this work in English (written originally in Latin about 1260) is dated 1495 (Trevisa's English translation of 1397). It was edited by Berthelet and published in London in 1535, and again by Batman in 1582. See Gerald E. Se Boyer, "Bartholomaeus Anglicus and His Encyclopedia," *JEGP,* xix (1920), 168–189; and Thorndike, *op. cit.,* ii, 405–406.

[31] *Le Compost* was published at Paris in 1493, and proved so popular (six editions before 1500) that it was translated into English three different times: in 1503, 1506, and 1508. The last and best of these editions was made by Robert Copland and printed by Wynkyn de Worde. It was reprinted at fairly frequent intervals throughout the sixteenth century—sixteen editions by 1618. I have used H. O. Sommer's excellent edition, *The Kalender of Shepherdes* (London, 1892), who prints the Paris edition of 1503 in photographic facsimile, a reprint of Pynson's edition of 1506, and provides a long critical introduction.

[32] Sommer, *op. cit.,* p. 144.

[33] *Ibid.,* p. 156. "Ptholomaeus" was supposed to be taken by the public to mean Claudius Ptolemy. See, however, *post,* note 35.

reader is instructed how to cast an elementary horoscope. First, he is given directions for discovering what planet governs the hour in which the child is born. Each of the twenty-four hours of the day is governed by a certain planet. Beginning with Sunday (i.e., midnight Saturday), and considering the planets always in the order of Sol, Venus, Mercury, Luna, Saturn, Jupiter, and Mars, the first hour of Sunday is ruled by Sol, the second hour by Venus, the third by Mercury, and so on. This will result in Luna ruling the first hour of Monday, Mars the first hour of Tuesday, Mercury the first of Wednesday, Jupiter the first of Thursday, Venus the first of Friday, and Saturn the first of Saturday. The child born in the hour governed by Sol shall be "prudent and wyse" and "a grete speker." Whoever is thus born under Mars is "a lyer / a thefe / a decyver / bygge and of reed coloure." And so on.

The reader who would learn more of his destiny by this particular method is advised to turn back to the "proprytees of the seven planettes afore reherced." Then there is provided a general horoscope for each month of the year, to be coupled, of course, with the characteristics bestowed upon one by his ruling planet "afore reherced." The paragraph concerning Pisces will serve as an example:

They that be borne under Pisces fro the myd Feveryere unto ye myd of Marche he shall be wyse and conynge / in many sciencs and shall go far and be a wedloke breker and a mocker and very covetous / he shall say one / & do another he shall fynde hyden money. He shall trust in his wysdome and shall defende wydowes and maydens / and motherlys chyldren / & shall passe very lyghtely all his troubles / & shall live lxxii yere / after nature. The woman that then is borne shall be delycyous / famulyer pleasaunt of corage and shall have grete sekenes in hir iyes and be sclanderyd and defamed. Hir husbande shall forsake hir / and with that she shall have great payne with strangeours and she shall nat have it that is hir owne / she shall have sekenes in hir stomake and in hir chyldebed / she shall leve lxxii yere after nature saterday & tuysday is to them evyll / as moche the man as the woman / and they shall lyve faythfully.[34]

These rough-and-ready horoscopes of *The Kalender* are just the sort of thing we may buy nowadays in the five-and-ten-cent-store astrology booklets entitled "Were You Born in August?", and contain only the merest gist of the complex system of astrology found in the works of Ptolemy and other "authorities." But the *Kalender's* numerous printings in sixteenth-century England indicate that much of the average man's knowledge of astrology must have been derived from this source. Furthermore, its astronomical and astrological portions were pirated about 1532 by Robert Wyer, the most flourishing English printer of small handbooks for the middle-classes, and printed in a booklet entitled *The Compost of Ptholomaeus, Prynce of Astronomye,* which became somewhat a "best seller" of

[34] Sommer, p. 165.

the first half of the century.[35] Other books of this period expounding astrological material of a similar nature were Erra Pater's *Book of Knowledge, Treating of the Wisdom of the Ancients*,[36] Thomas Moulton's *Myrrour or Glasse of Helthe*,[37] and Dr. Andrew Boorde's *Pryncyples of Astronamye*.[38]

Middle-class Englishmen in the first half of the sixteenth century obtained from such books just enough astrology to be fascinated by it without learning a great deal about it as a science of intricate manifestations. The publishing houses of the Continent were pouring forth the astrology texts of Ptolemy, the Arabians, and sixteenth-century astrologers which no doubt many an Englishman purchased; but no one had produced in English an elaborate astrology textbook, and no important astrology textbook, in any language, had been printed in England.

After 1550, however, more and more English writings on astrology appeared, and several Continental treatises on the subject were Englished and published in London. Anthony Ascham published a *Treatise of Astronomie, declaring . . . the influence of the planets, signs and constellations* (1550, 1552, 1559). In 1557 a work of Oronce Fine was translated and issued by Humphrey Baker as *A Briefe and Short Introduction to Judiciall Astrology* (reprinted in 1587). In 1558 Dr. John Dee published a book of astrological Aphorisms and Cyprianus Leovitius issued in London his *Brevis judicandi genituras*, affixed to which was Hieronymus Wolf's *Admonitio de vero astrologiae usu*. Leovitius' *De conjunctionibus magnis insignioribus superiorum planetarum* (first published at Lauginae in 1564) was printed in London in 1573. In the 1570's and 1580's London saw the publication of numerous treatises on the comet of 1577 and the great conjunction of Saturn and Jupiter in 1583.[39] Later there appeared Robert Tanner's *Mirror for Mathematiques . . . for Astronomers and Astrologians* (1587), Erra Pater's

[35] See H. B. Lathrop, "Some Rogueries of Robert Wyer," *The Library*, 3rd Series, v (1914), 349–364, an article that dispels the previously held notion that Wyer's *Compost* is culled from Ptolemy's *Centiloquium*. Cf. also Francis R. Johnson, *Astronomical Thought in Renaissance England* (Baltimore, 1937), p. 75. The *Short-Title Catalogue* lists printings of the *Compost* in 1532?, 1535?, 1540?, 1635?

[36] The *STC* lists this under Godfridus rather than Erra Pater, but William Lilly's edition of it (New York, 1794) ascribes it Erra Pater. It appeared in 1530?, 1585?, and 1619.

[37] This was indeed a "best seller," as the fourteen printings before 1580 listed in the *STC* will attest.

[38] Cf. *The Fyrst Boke of the Introduction of Knowledge*, ed. F. J. Furnivall, *EETS, ES*, x, although Furnivall does not reprint the astrological portions. The only copy of the original of 1547 is in Trinity College, Cambridge.

[39] See especially in Bibliography items under Hill, Fleming, Nausea, Hooker, Tanner, Twyne, Harvey, Bariona, and Shakelton.

(or Godfridus') *Boke of Knowledge apperteynge to Astronomye* (1588), John Blagrave's *Astrolabium Uranicum Generale . . . with all such neces-sary Supplements for Judiciall Astrology as Alkabitius and Claudius have Delivered* (1596), and Nathaniel Torporley's *Valve Astronomicae Uni-versales* (1602). None of these, however, are as important as the astrology textbooks produced on the Continent. English publishers apparently con-centrated more upon almanacks, astrological prognostications of various sorts, treatises on particularly notable astronomical or astrological events.

In 1558 and many times subsequently, however, appeared Fabian Withers' translation of John Indagine's textbook entitled *Briefe Introductions . . . in Natural Astrology*. Although not astrologically a very imposing work, and not presenting the orthodox astrology of Ptolemy, Maternus, and the Arabians, it was evidently a somewhat popular book. Only Books II and III deal with astrology. Book II explains chiefly the influence of the Sun in each face (i.e., each 10 degrees) of each sign of the zodiac. The Sun in the first ten degrees of Aries, says Indagine,

doth commonly make those which be then born, red-colored, small visaged, lank and slender bodies, and leane, marked in the left foot or elbow, having many friends, hating evill, and loving all that is good.

In the second face, which is the tenth degree of Aries to the twenty degree of the same, it maketh them black colored, . . . They be also of civilitie, angry, suspicious, deceitful, and hartie, compassed and beset with many enemies, which shall pursue him even unto death.

In the third face it maketh them oftentimes red, inclining to a saffron colour, solitary, and devising craftes and deceipts.[40]

And so on for each of the other signs. The remainder of Book II is con-cerned with the qualities of the planets and their aspects, the signs and triplicities, and the illnesses governed by each of the signs of the zodiac.

Book III is "A Compendious description of Natural Astrology." Accord-ing to Indagine, "natural" astrology is that which considers only the posi-tion of the Sun and the lord of the sign the Sun is in at one's birth, to be distinguished from "artificial" astrology which considers the sign actually rising on the horizon and the actual positions of all the planets. In describ-ing the erection of the horoscope,[41] Indagine tells us that if Aries is the sign the Sun is in at birth,[42] Aries is placed in the first house of the horo-scope, Taurus in the second house, Gemini in the third, and so on, accord-ing to the natural order of the signs. In such a figure, Mars is placed in the first house (because Mars governs Aries), and the other planets are thus placed arbitrarily ("and contrarye to Firmicus") in the horoscope according to what Indagine calls their "natural" order (i.e., Sol, Venus, Mercury,

[40] Sig. H5v. (1575 ed., Folger Shakespeare Library copy).
[41] Sigs. P3r ff.
[42] Which always means, of course, that the birthday is between the middle of March and the middle of April.

Luna, Saturn, Jupiter, Mars); that is, Sol in the second house, Venus in the third, Mercury in the fourth, and so on. After erecting the figure for a nativity in this fashion (which should have horrified an astrologer because it disregards the *actual* positions of the planets in the heavens), the reader may interpret his "horoscope with Aries in the ascendant" as follows:

This Horoscope maketh them which are borne, glorifying in youth, without brethren, or one at the most, if they be fortunate: having a mutable inheritance, now gotten, and now lost, and strait recovered again, inclined to the diseases of the head rather than to any other sicknesse. . . . For the most part bestowing his labor and good wil upon unthankful persons. . . .

Capricorne in the midst of the heaven, doth discern honors, riches, promotions, secrets of religion, and a suttle wit. Libra in the west sheweth the life and courtly maners, the which life few do allow: for it is unconstant, calling down a man from honor and reputation, into infamie and reproch: fortune now flattering and laughing upon him, and by and by vexing him with sundry miseries and calamities. . . . But all these evils whatsoever they are, Cancer in the nether part of the heaven doth amende and recompense.[43]

Further on in the book he may find additional information:

The Sun being in Aries, maketh them which are borne, neither riche, neither very poore. Also angry, but sone pleased, studious, eloquent, diverse, proud, lying, and luxurious, promising (as they say) mountaines of gold, and performing nothinge, evil reported of amongst his kindred, and shall be broughte in daunger by his enemies, which shall be men of power. He shall be hurte by foure footed beastes, as being cast off a horse, he shall receive great woundes with daunger of death. So much unfortunate and advers shall all kinde of hawking, hunting, fighting, and al things to be done on horsebacke be, and happen unto him: in other thinges he shal be more fortunate and happy, and also long lived. Also if it be a maid which is borne she shal be given to lying, angry, faire, curious, delitinge in new and strange things, envious and fruitful in children, whose first child shall be slaine, she shal be in many perils and daungers, whereby she shal get a marke or star in the head, or els be naturally marked there, or in the feete. This we have noted also out of certain authors, that the children of Aries, being borne in the day, shalbe fortunate and of great reputation and renowine amongst greate men and princes; contraiwise, they which are borne in the night, to be unfortunate, and of no reputation.[44]

In 1562 (and many times subsequently) appeared William Warde's translation of a strange volume entitled *The Most Excellent, Profitable, and Pleasaunt Boke of the Famous Doctor and Expert Astrologian Arcandam or Aleandrin, to Find the Fatal Destiny, Complexion, and Natural Inclination of Every Man and Child, by His Birth.*[45] The book opens abruptly

---

[43] Sigs. L6v–L7v.    [44] Sigs. N2r–N3v.

[45] This book is recorded in the *STC* as appearing in 1562?, 1578, 1592, 1626, 1630, 1634, and 1637. Continental publications of it (Latin or French) appeared in 1541, 1542, 1553, 1575, 1576, 1584, 1587, 1615, and 1625. This seems to be a badly garbled translation of the mediaeval manuscript by Alhandrei mentioned by Thorndike, I, 710–716, and Sarton, I, 671. Cf. Dee's list, *supra,* item 24.

with a discussion of nativities. The author's peculiar method of determining the sign under which a person is born is based upon a numerical calculation of the value of the child's name and that of his mother. The letters in these two names which correspond to the ancient Roman figures are given the corresponding numerical values; the sum of these is divided by 29 and the result determines the zodiacal mansion governing the birth. Arcandam expresses it thus:

If yee will know the constellation of any man, take his natural name, which is commonly called his proper name, and the proper name of his mother. . . . Then diligently consider every letter of the sayde two names and amongst the same, gather the numerical letters, such as signifies a number which according to the ancient accompt are seven. I signifieth one, V five, X tenne, L fifty, C hundred, D five hundred, M signifieth a thousand. Taking all the singular letters of the said two names as well the number, as such as signifie a number. Then gather the whole summe, which summe so collected divide, if it be possible, by XXIX because of the XXIX constellations and Starres, which after the ancient manner is the first division of the Signs. And hereby it appeareth, that the principall parts of the particular starres and signs celestial in number are XXIX, as hereafter shall appear. Sometimes the sayde number doth amount just to the summe of XXIX and sometimes exceedeth the same, wherein it is to be noted, that either the number doth exceed or else is equal. If it exceed, then the number ought to be applyed and divided by their unities to the sayde figures, beginning at the first signe which is the head of Aries, and so the rest successively. Than whatsoever the last unitie of this number shall rest or remaine, that is the special signe as is of most force in the time of the nativitie.[46]

Here is confusion and obscurity indeed, but Arcandam proceeds to discuss fully the destinies of those born under each of the various signs of the zodiac. He begins with the physical qualities of the "native," gives his moral characteristics, his health and sickness, his term of life, his lucky days, the number of his children, the manner of his death. Those born under the first part of Aries are "yellow colored, small bellied, nimble and straight, thin and lean of body"; have a mark or sign on the left foot; lose and recover again their inheritance; have many friends; are "subtile, politic, and craftye"; are "prone to pains in the head" but otherwise of good health. Those born under the second part of Aries shall be very hairy, have a great beard, "colored eyes" (!), "white teeth, fair nose, great eyebrows of color red mixed with saffron color"; they shall be "eloquent, solitary, . . . prodigal, deceitful, and prone to hurt other; they shall be ireful, greatly given to vice," possess many enemies, and have "a stripe" in their face made probably by a sword; they shall "waxe sick at 30 years," but "be happy in tillage." [47] As far as orthodox astrology is concerned, Arcandam's work is

[46] Sigs. A3r–A4v (1634 edition, Folger Shakespeare Library copy).
[47] Sigs. B1r–B2r.

of very little importance; yet the number of editions published indicates that it was widely read in Elizabethan England. I suspect the title was attractive.

In 1583 and 1593 respectively appeared two works of a more authoritative calibre: Claudius Dariot's continentally popular work was translated by Fabian Withers as *A Briefe Introduction to the Astrologicall Judgement of the Starres* (1583, 1591, 1598, 1653), and Augier Ferrier's equally popular text was translated by Thomas Kelway as *A Learned Astronomical Discourse of the Judgement of Nativities* (1593, 1642).[48] After discussing the basic principles and terms of the science, together with the qualities and influences of the planets, Dariot proceeds to direct one in the method of erecting a horoscope by means of the Ephemerides, and to illustrate his discussion with an example configuration. He explains such intricate phases of the horoscope as the "Part of Life," the "Part of Fortune," "The Part of Death," and the "Killing Planet." The next third of his book is a series of chapters concerning astrological *interrogations,* and the last third is comprised of four chapters on *elections.*

The comprehensiveness of Ferrier's *Astronomical Discourse* may be best perceived by observing its Table of Contents:

## THE FIRST BOOKE

Of the Celestial figure of a Nativitie.
Of the verification of the houre of the Nativitie.
The manner to sette downe the saide figure verified.
Of the parts of Nativities.
Of the latitudes and aspects of the Planets.
Of the fortunes and infortunes of Planets, and parts of heaven.
If the Child shall lyve or no.
Of the gyver of life, called of the Arabians *Alcocoden.*
Of them that augment and diminish the number of the sayd yeeres.
Of the Lord of the nativity.
Of the understanding and maners of the man
Of riches and poverty.
Of what meanes riches and poverty come.
Of the time that the riches & damages shall come.
Of brethren
Of Father and Mother.
Of heritages and goods of the earth.
Of Chyldren.
Of servaunts.
Of Diseases.
Of marriage.
Of Dowrey and other goods by meanes of marriage.
Of the death.

[48] For Latin and French editions, see Bibliography.

Of voyages by Land and by Sea.
Of the constancie of his religion.
Of the action and profesion.
Of dignities, offices and honours.
Of companions and friends.
Of sutes and enemies.
Of imprisonments and captivities.
Of horses, Muttons, and other beasts.

### THE SECOND BOOKE

Of the significations of the Planets.
Of the significations of the twelve signes.
Of that which the Plannets signifie in the sayd signes.
Of the aspects of the Planets between them.
Of the significations of the twelve houses.
Of the Lords of the Triplicities of the saide houses.
What the Plannets signifie in the twelve houses.
The significations of the Lords of the houses, by all the places of the figure.

### THE THIRD BOOKE

Of Directions.
Of the Seperator or Burner, called of the Arabians *Algebuthar.*
Of the Lords of the Tryplicities.
Of Revolutions.
Of the judgements upon the Revolutions.
Of the yeeres governed by the Planets, called by the Arabians *Fridarie.*
Of Profections.
The Lord of the circulation, from the Lorde of the hower of the nativity.
Of the circulation of the Lorde of the ascendant, and of the Planets which be in
    the ascendant.
Of the Eclipses and great conjunctions appertayning to the Revolutions of
    nativities.
Of the particular meetings of all the yeere.[49]

Dariot and Ferrier had plucked out some of the heart of Ptolemy's and
Albohazen Haly's astrological mystery, and their English translators had
presented it for the layman in a tongue he could readily understand.

There were also books printed in English and published in London
treating especially of the use of astrology in medical practice. In 1583 John
Harvey translated and published Hermes Trismegistus' *Iatromathematica,*
which delineated the parts of the body which each planet governed and the
types of diseases over which each planet had dominion. In the 1598 edition
of Dariot's *Briefe Introduction to . . . the Starres,* one "G. C." appended
a comprehensive *Treatise of Mathematical Physicke;* and in 1606 John

[49] Folger Shakespeare Library copy.

Fage's *Speculum Aegrotorum: the Sicke-mens Glasse* presented an elaborate exposition of medical astrology.[50]

Sometimes annexed to the common almanack of the sixteenth century, and sometimes issued separately, was the astrological Prognostication. These pamphlets prophesied any unusual happenings resultant from such phenomena as eclipses, comets, and conjunctions of the planets, regarding such things as crops, epidemics, war, politics, and so on; and in addition provided certain astrological rules for phlebotomy, bathing, sowing seeds, travel, buying and selling. Sometimes these Prognostications predicted events for forty years to come, but mostly they interpreted merely a single year's planetary manifestations. Vaughan's *Almanack and Prognostication for 1559,* for example, tells thus of the malefic events to occur in that year:

> The conjunction of Saturne and Mars in this eclipse, signifieth dessencions, discordes, contencions, stryfe, great manslaughter, murmuracions, feares, and troubles shall happen to men, and no pytie nor mercy almost among men. . . .
>
> Also Saturne, Mars, Sol and Luna, in Tauro decimo domo, domus honoris, will not leave this yere without augmentinge of moche discorde and noughty enterprises, producing descension, betwene the higher powers, and the lower or meaner sorte, betwene the spiritualty and the temporaltie with moche pillage, theftes, robberies, murmuracions, lyes, great noyses, tumultes, comocions, and such outrages. . . .
>
> The Figure of the heavens, at the time of the Eclipse of the Moone, 1559 . . . signifieth great mischief, discorde, manslaughter, hatred and wrath, aswel private as public, with deceit, treason, theft, burynge, adulterye, robberie, and finally all kind of wickednes. Also betwene secular riche and mighty princes, warre, envy, hatred, rancour, and deceit. Also the officers of great estate of some great prince shalbe deposed of their offyce, and shalbe greatlye hated of their prince.[51]

Similar Prognostications were issued throughout the century. A notable series of such pamphlets regarding the great conjunction of Saturn and Jupiter in 1583 were published in London that year; and apparently another series was issued at the turn of the century remarking the extraordinary celestial phenomena during the first few years of the seventeenth century. It was chiefly this type of publication which kept especially alive the idea that eclipses, comets, planetary revolutions, and conjunctions foreboded famine, pestilence, the death of great ones, and evil happenings generally.[52]

[50] I have used the Folger Shakespeare Library and the Library of Congress copies of these three works. For an interesting and informing account of such astrological medicine, see Carroll Camden, Jr., "Elizabethan Astrological Medicine," *Annals of Medical History,* II (1930), 217–226.

[51] Sigs. A3r, A5r, B2v–B3v; cited by F. S. Larkey, "Astrology and Politics in the First Years of Elizabeth's Reign," *Bulletin of the Institute of the History of Medicine,* III (1935), p. 176.

[52] Much has been written in recent years concerning these popular booklets of the sixteenth and seventeenth centuries. Note especially Eustace F. Bosanquet,

In this chapter we have sketched briefly the development of astrology textbooks from ancient times through the mediaeval centuries, noticing the significant works (and occasionally their contents) which the Renaissance inherited from its mediaeval ancestors, together with those works of the sixteenth century which appeared as new. Emphasized has been the dissemination of astrological knowledge through the medium of the printing press, the various editions and the apparent popularity of these works being especially noted and considered. Although we may now have at least an idea of what the sixteenth-century Englishman had to draw upon to piece out his astrological knowledge, an examination of all the works listed in the Bibliography which follows would give us a much more complete picture. It is to the Bibliography itself (in section V) that the reader is especially commended.

## IV

The most comprehensive bibliographies of early-printed astrological works are those compiled by Robert Watt,[1] J. C. Brunet,[2] J. C. Houzeau and A. Lancaster,[3] A. Bouche-Leclercq,[4] F. L. Gardner,[5] Franz Cumont,[6] and Robert Peddie.[7] Each of these impressive collections contains items not found in the others, and all fail to mention many items discovered in still other sources—doubtless because a complete bibliography of works concerned in any way with astrology is virtually impossible to compile. The subject, with all of its ramifications, is too large.

*English Printed Almanacks and Prognostications: A Bibliographical History to the Year 1600* (London, 1917); "English Printed Almanacks and Prognostications: Corregenda and Addenda," *The Library,* 4th Series, VIII (1928), 456–477; "English Seventeenth-Century Almanacks," *The Library,* 4th Series, X (1930), 361–397; "Leonard Digges and His Books," *Oxford Bibliographical Society Proceedings and Papers,* I, 247–252; Carroll Camden, Jr., "Elizabethan Almanacs and Prognostications," *The Library,* 4th Series, XII (1931–32), 83–108, 194–207; E. P. Wilson, "Some English Mock-Prognostications," *The Library,* 4th Series, XIX (1939), 6–43; M. Rene Pruvost, "The Astrological Prognostications in 1583," *The Library,* 4th Series, XIV (1934), 101–106; F. S. Larkey, *op. cit.;* and notes on the prognostications of 1583 in R. B. McKerrow, *The Works of Thomas Nashe* (London, 1905), v.

[1] *Bibliothetica Britannica* (Edinburgh, 1824).

[2] *Manuel du Libraire et de l'Amateur de Livres* (Paris, 1860–80).

[3] *Bibliographie Generale de l'Astronomie* (Brussels, 1882–89).

[4] *L'Astrologie Grecque* (Paris, 1899).

[5] *A Catalogue Raisonne of Works on the Occult Sciences* (London, 1903–12), II, III.

[6] *Catalogus codicum astrologorum graecorum* (London, 1920).

[7] *A Subject Index of Books Published before 1800* (London, 1933–39).

I have found indispensable information in the pages and footnotes of
Lynn Thorndike's monumental six volumes entitled *A History of Magic
and Experimental Science* (New York, 1923–41), and in George Sarton's
two-volume *Introduction to the History of Science* (Baltimore, 1927–31).
Ten pages of astrological bibliography is at the end of William Lilly's
*Christian Astrology* (London, 1647), and an equally imposing array of
past authorities is in Francis Junctin's *Speculum Astrologiae* (Lyons, 1581).
I have also checked the card-files of the Library of Congress, the Folger
Shakespeare Library, the Library of the U. S. Surgeon General; and pored
over the *British Museum Catalogue,* the *Bibliotheque Nationale,* Hain-
Copinger's *Repertorium Bibliographicum,* Pollard and Redgrave's *Short-
Title Catalogue.* And for a few items I have used several less important
sources.

The following bibliography is a list of books (and their separate editions)
on the subject of astrology published between 1473 and 1625. It includes,
however, only those works which inform of the principles or techniques of
the science—the textbooks of the subject, so to speak. It does not include
works devoted, for example, to the controversy over astrology's validity—a
subject beyond the scope of the present work and one which is treated particularly well in D. C. Allen's *The Star-Crossed Renaissance* (Durham,
1941). Excluded is the vast number of almanack-prognostications, which
have been listed by the hundreds in the publications of E. F. Bosanquet,
especially in his *English Printed Almanacks and Prognostications . . . to
1600* (London, 1917). Excluded also are Ephemerides or planetary tables,
treatises on a special event such as a particular eclipse, a particular conjunction of certain planets—unless these perchance give considerable information on actual astrological techniques. Nor have I listed more than a few of
the numerous treatises on the appearances of comets. Had I not made these
exclusions, the bibliography which follows would have left little space in
the book for anything else.

No doubt I have occasionally violated these rules of inclusion and ex-
clusion. Bibliography is difficult when one cannot have at hand each book
he lists; and although I have actually handled many of the items cited, for
others I have had to depend upon what other writers and compilers have
had to say about their contents. Nevertheless, it is a fairly complete list of
books containing the principles and techniques of astrology as they were
promulgated during the years 1473–1625. The list will serve one of its
purposes if it connotes to the reader an idea of the voluminousness of works
on astrology printed in the Renaissance. One can hardly look even cursorily
at such a list and still maintain that astrology existed in the Renaissance
only for a few who were particularly gullible and superstitious.

I have not considered necessary detailed collation or a listing of different
titles of the same book. Although Alchabitius' *Libellus introductorius
isagogicus judicorum astrorum* of 1473 was entitled *Astrologiae judiciariae*

*principia* in 1525, these were virtually the same text; consequently in such instances one title has been listed, followed by places and dates of publication of subsequent editions.

## V

Abraham ibn Ezra (Judeus). *Liber de nativitatibus . . . judiciariam astrologiam.* Venice, 1484, 1485; Augsburg, 1491; Cologne, 1537; Rome, 1545.
——. *De luminaribus et diebus criticis liber.* Lyons, 1496, 1508; Rome, 1544; Lyons, 1550; Frankfort, 1614.
——. *In re judiciali opera.* Venice, 1507. (Seven separate treatises.)
Adam, P. *Horologia.* N.p., 1500?
Aegidius de Wissekerke (Willem Gilliszoon). *Liber desideratus super celestium motuum indagatione sine calculo.* Lyons, 1494; Cremona, n.d.
Aevolus, Caesar. *De causis antipathiae et sympathiae rerum naturalium.* Venice, 1580.
Agrippa, Henry Cornelius (von Nettesheim). *De occulta philosophia libri tres.* Paris, 1531 (Bk. I only); Antwerp, 1531 (Bk. I only); Lyons, 1531 (Bk. I only); Cologne, 1532, 1533; Basle, 1565, 1567; Cologne, 1580; Basle, 1583.
Ailly, Petrus de. *Concordancia astronomiae cum theologia.* Augsburg, 1490; Venice, 1494.
Aitfingerus, Michael. *Pentaplus regnorum mundi.* Antwerp, 1579.
Albenait. (See *Liber.*)
Albertus Magnus. *Speculum astronomiae.* Venice, 1517; Lyons, 1615.
Albinius, P. Constantius (de Villanova). *Magia astrologica, hoc est, clavis sympathiae septem mettalorum et septem selectorum lapidum ad planetas.* Paris, 1611. (Cf. *Arlensis.*)
Albohazen Haly filius Abenragel (Alboacen). *Liber completus in judiciis astrorum.* Venice, 1485, 1503, 1520, 1523; N.p., 1525; Basle, n.d., 1551, 1571.
——. *De revolutionibus nativitatum.* Venice, 1524.
Albohali. *De judiciis nativitatum liber* (or *Albohali Arabis astrologi. . . .*). Nuremberg, 1546, 1549.
——. (See *Liber.*)
Albubather (Abu Bakr). *Liber de nativitatibus.* Venice, 1492, 1493, 1501, 1510; Nuremburg, 1540.
Albumasar. *Introductorium in astronomiam.* Augsburg, 1485?, 1489; Venice, 1489, 1490, 1495; Augsburg, 1495; Venice, 1506, 1515.
——. *De magnis conjunctionibus et annorum revolutionibus.* Augsburg, 1489, 1495; Venice, 1503, 1506, 1515.
——. *Flores astrologiae.* Augsburg, 1488; Venice, 1488, 1490, 1495; Augsburg, 1495; Venice, n.d., 1515.

Alchabitius. *Libellus introductorius isagogicus judicorum astrorum.* Bononiae, 1473; Venice, 1481, 1482, 1485, 1491, 1502, 1503, 1505, 1511, 1512, 1513; Paris, 1521 (three eds.), 1524; Lyons, 1525, n.d.; Paris, 1557; Cologne, 1560; Rome, 1585.

Aliegri, F. di. *Tratato di astrologia e de la chieromancie.* Venice, 1501.

Alkindi. *Astrorum indices, de pluviis, imbribus et ventis, ac aeris mutatione.* Venice, 1507, 1509.

Almansor. *Liber nonus.* Venice, 1497.

Alsted, John Henry. *Cursus philosophici encyclopedia libris xxvii.* . . . Herborn, 1620, 1630.

Alvarez, Antonio. *Epistolarum et consiliorum medicinalium.* Naples, 1585.

Ampsingius, Johannes Assverus. *Dissertatio iatromathematica.* Rostock, 1602, 1618.

Andrelini, Fausto. *De influentia syderum.* Paris, 1496.

Anonymous. (See end of list.)

Aomer. (See *Liber.*)

Aquivivus, A. M. *Libri quatuor* . . . *astrologiae.* Helenopoli, 1609.

Arcandam (Alhandrei, etc.). *De veritatibus et praedictionibus astrologiae.* Paris, 1541, 1542, 1553.

——. *Livre d'Arcandam traictant des predictions de l'astrologie.* Paris, 1575; Lyons, 1576; Rouen, 1584; Lyons, 1587; Paris, 1615; Lyons, 1625.

——. *The Most Excellent Booke of Arcandam, to Finde the Fatall Destiny of Every Man.* Trans. William Warde. London, 1562?, 1578, 1592, 1617, 1626.

Archimedes. *De constitutione horoscopii.* Basle, 1563.

Aristotle. (See *Liber.*)

Arlensis, Petrus (de Scudalupis). *De sympathia septem metallorum ac septem selectorum lapidum ad planetas.* Rome, 1595; Matriti, 1598; Paris, 1610, 1611. (Cf. *Albinius.*)

Arma, J. F. *De significatione stellae crinitae.* Taurini, 1578.

Artephius. *De characteribus planetarum.* Frankfort, 1615?

Ascham, Anthony. *Treatise of Astronomie, declaring* . . . *the influence of the Planets, Signs and Constellations.* London, 1550, 1552, 1559.

Baffius, J. B. V. *De Cometis libri tres.* Perusiae, 1580, 1585.

——. *Libellus de non usu astrologiae in medicina.* Perugiae, 1595?

Baker, Humphrey. *Introduction to Judiciall Astrologie.* London, 1557?, 1587.

Bandorkowic, J. *Quaestio de actione coeli in haec inferiora.* Cracoviae, 1621.

Bariona, Laurentius. *Cometographia.* London, 1578.

Barrios, J. de. *De la verdadera cirugia, medicina y astrologia.* Madrid?, 1607.

Baranzanus, Redemptus. *Uranoscopia.* N.p., 1617.

Bartholinus, Caspar. *Astrologia seu de stellarum natura, affectionibus et effectionibus.* Wittenburg, 1606, 1607, 1609; Hafniae, 1611; Strassburg,

1612; Hafniae, 1616; Rostock, 1616; Hafniae, 1620, 1624; Strassburg, 1624.

Bartholomaeus Angelicus. *De proprietatibus rerum.* Cologne, 1472?; Basle, 1475?; Lyons, 1480; Cologne, 1481; Lyons, 1482 (2 eds.); Cologne, 1483; Nuremberg, 1483; Strassburg, 1485; Heidelberg, 1488; Strassburg, 1491; Nuremberg, 1492; London, 1495; Strassburg, 1505; Nuremberg, 1519; London, 1535, 1582; Frankfort, 1601. (Editions of 1495, 1535, and 1582 are English translations.)

Bassantinus, J. *Super mathematica genethliaca.* Lyons, 1560?

Bellanti, Lucio. *De astrologica veritate.* Bologna, 1495; Florence, 1498; Venice, 1502; Basle, 1554.

Belot, Jean. *Instruction . . . pour apprendre les sciences de chiromance et phisiognomie . . . plus un Discours astrologique.* Paris, 1619.

Bethem. *De significatione triplicitatum ortus.* Venice, 1484, 1493, 1519.

——. *De consuetudinibus in judiciis astrorum.* Venice, 1507.

Biondi, Michel Angelo. *De cognitione hominis per aspectum.* Rome, 1544.

——. *Tabulae annuae de anticipatione stellarum fixarum cum suis significationibus in disponendis vel constituendis operibus humanis.* Rome, 1544.

——. *Ex libris Hippocratis de nova et prisca arte medendi deque diebus decretoriis epitome.* Rome, 1545; Lyons, 1550; Francofurti, 1614.

Bodier, Thomas. *De ratione et usu dierum criticorum opus.* Paris, 1555.

Bonatus, Guido. *Liber astronomicus.* Augsburg, 1491; Venice, 1506; Basle, 1530, 1550, 1572; Augsburg, 1581.

Bonaventura, Fredericus. *Meteorological assertiones, . . . sive de causis et signis pluviarum, ventorum, serenitatis et tempestatum, de stellarum significationibus.* Venice, 1594; Urbini, 1595.

Bonincontrius, Laurentius. *De rebus coelestibus.* Venice, 1526; Basle, 1540, 1575.

——. *Tractatus astrologicus electionum.* Nuremburg, 1539.

——. *Opus de revolutionibus annorum.* Rome, 1491, 1505?

Boorde, Andrew. *The Pryncyples of Astronamye.* London, 1547.

Brugis, Joannes de. *Tractatus qui de veritate astronomie.* Antwerp, 1503; Venice, 1544.

Brunfels, Otto. *De definitationibus et terminis astrologiae libellus isagogicus.* Basle, 1533, 1551.

C., G. *A Treatise of Mathematicall Phisicke, or Briefe Introduction to Phisicke by Judiciall Astronomy.* London, 1598. (See *Dariot.*)

Camerarius, Joachiam. *Astrologica (Ex Hephaestione Alliusque Antiquis).* Nuremburg, 1532. (Contains also *Iatromathematica* of Hermes Trismegistus.)

——. *Cl. Ptolomaei de judiciis astrologicis libri iiii.* Basle, 1533; Nuremberg, 1535; Basle, 1540, 1541, 1551.

Camerarius, J. Rudolphus. *Centuriae dua geniturarum* (or *Horarium natalium . . . centuriae duae*). Frankfort, 1607, 1610, 1611; Amsterdam, 1633.

Cardan, Jerome (Geronomo, Hieronomo, etc.). *Aphorismorum astronomicorum segmenta septem; Liber de judiciis geniturarum*. Ulma, 1541.

——. *Libello Duo: Unus De supplemento almanach, Alter De restitutione temporum et motuum coelestium; Item Geniturae LXVII insignes casibus et fortuna cum expositione*. Nuremburg, 1543, 1547.

——. *Libelli Quinque: De supplemento almanach, De restitutione temporum et motuum coelestium; De judiciis geniturarum; De revolutionibus; De exemplis centum geniturarum; Item aphorismorum astronomicorum segmenta VII*. Nuremburg, 1547.

——. *In Cl. Ptolomaei libros iv de astrorum judiciis; De VII erraticarum stellarum qualitatibus atque viribus; Geniturarum item XII exempla; De interrogationibus libellus*. Basle, 1553/1554; Lyons, 1555; Basle, 1559, 1579, 1583. (Last edition containing also *De planetis de Cardan* and *Tabula in Ptolemei Apotelesmata de Dasypodius*.)

——. *De malo recentiorum medicorum medendi usu*. Venice, 1545.

——. *Contradicentium medicorum liber*. Venice, 1545.

——. *De libris propriis eorumque ordine et usu ac de mirabilibus operibus in arte medica factis*. Lyons, 1557.

——. *Liber de providentia anni constitutione; in septem aphorismorum Hippocratis particulas*. Basle, 1564.

——. *Opera omnia*. Lyons, 1663. 10 vols.

Carion, Johannes. *De effectibus directionum*. Frankfort, 1611.

Cartagensis, Antonius. *Liber de peste, de signis febrium et de diebus criticis*. N.p., 1531?

Cheyne, James. *Orationes duo de perfecto philosopho et de praedicationibus astrologorum*. Doway, 1577.

Cimbrus, Elias Olaus. *Diarium astrologicum . . . et De Cometa*. Uraniburgae, 1586.

Cirvelo, Pedro Sanches. *Apotelesmata astrologiae Christianiae*. Alcala, 1521.

Claudius, Caesar. *De diebus criticis*. Basle, 1620.

Codronchus, Baptista. *De annis climactericis*. Cologne, 1623.

Coelestinus, Claudius. *De influentiis coelorum*. Paris, 1542.

Compost. (See *Kalender*.)

Corella, A. de. *Secretos de filosofia, astrologia y medicina*. Valladolid, 1546; Sarragoza, 1547.

Cortes, Geronimo. *Phisonomia. . . .* Cordova, 1601; Zaragoza, 1603; Tarragona, 1609, 1610, 1614.

Creutzer, P. *Planeten Buchlein*. Frankfort, 1548; N.p., 1553.

Curtius, Matthaeus. *Tractationes medicinales*. Venice, 1562.

Curtius, Joachimus (Joachim Cureus?). *Commentatio de certitudine matheseos et astronomiae cum decisione quaestionis astrologicae*. Hamburg, 1618.

Dariot, Claudius. *Ad astrorum judicia facilis introductio. De morbis et diebus criticis ex astrorum motu cognoscendis fragmentum.* Lyons, 1557, 1582.

——. *L'Introduction facile aux jugements des astres.* Lyons, 1558, 1589.

——. *De la connaissance des maladies et des jours critiques d'apres le mouvement des astres.* Lyons, 1582.

——. *A Briefe and Most Easie Introduction to the Astrologicall Judgement of the Starres. Translated lately by Fabian Withers. Added A Treatise of Mathematical Physicke by G. C.* London, 1583, 1591, 1598, 1653 (last edition entitled *Dariotus Redivivus*).

Dasypodius (Rauchfuss), Conrad. *Brevis doctrina de cometis et cometarum effectibus.* Strassburg, 1578.

Dee, John. *Propaedeumata aphoristica de praestantioribus quibusdam naturae virtutibus.* London, 1558.

Diedo, G. B. *L'Anatomia celeste, . . . astrologica.* Venice, 1593/1594.

Dietericus, Helvicus. *Elogium planetarum.* Strassburg, 1627.

Dolingius, J. *Astrologia naturalis.* Gryphiswaldiae, 1613.

Dorn, Gerard. *Clavis totius philosophiae chymisticae.* Lyons, 1566.

——. *Compendium astronomiae.* Lyons?, 1584.

Dorotheus. (See *Liber.*)

Ehinger, E. *Judicium astrologicum von dem newen Cometen.* Augsburg, 1619; Venice, 1619.

Eisenmenger. (See *Siderocrates.*)

Engel, John (Johannes Angelus). *Astrolabium planum.* Augsburg, 1488; Venice, 1494.

Eschuid, John (John Eschendon). *Summa astrologiae judicialis.* Venice, 1489.

Essler, Joannes. *Speculum astrologicum.* Mainz, 1508; Basle, 1568, 1573, 1575, 1596.

——. *Theorica planetarum et octave sphaerae.* Basle, 1509.

Etzler, August. *Introductorium iatromathematicum.* N.p., 1622.

Fabre, Claude. *Paraphrasis.* Lyons, 1550. (Astrological medicine)

Fabricus, Jacobus. *Prognosis astrologica.* Halle, 1602.

Fage, John. *Speculum Aegrotorum: the Sicke-Mens Glasse. . . .* London, 1606, 1638.

Fernel, Jean. *Universa medicina.* N.p., 1567.

Ferrier, Augier (Oger). *Les jugemens astronomiques sur les nativitez.* Lyons, 1550; Paris, 1555; Lyons, 1582, 1583; Rouen, 1583.

——. *De diebus decretoriis.* Lyons, 1541, 1549; Leyden, 1549; Lyons, 1574, 1602.

——. *A Learned Astronomical Discourse of the Judgement of Nativities. . . .* Trans. Thomas Kelway. London, 1593, 1642.

Ferrerius, J. *De vera cometae significatione.* Paris, 1540; Florence, 1577, 1618.

Feselius, P. *Grundtlicher discurs von der astrologia judiciaria.* Strassburg, 1609.

Ficino, Marsiglio. *De vita coelitus comparanda.* Venice, 1484; Florence, 1489.

——. *De triplici vita, libri tres.* Florence, 1490; Bononiae, 1501; Strassburg, 1511; Venice, 1525; Basle, 1532; Paris, 1547; Lyons, 1560.

——. *Opera.* Basle, 1561.

Finaeus, Orontius (Oronce Fine). *Briefve . . . introduction . . . sur la judiciaire astrologie.* . . . Paris, 1538, 1543, 1551, 1556.

——. *De xii coeli comiciliis.* Lutetiae, 1553.

Finarensis, David. *L'Epitome de la vraye astrologie.* Paris, 1547.

Finckii, Thomas. *Horoscopographia.* . . . Slesvici, 1591.

Fiornouvellus, J. M. *Opusculum de cometis.* Ferrarae, 1578.

Firmicus. (See *Maternus.*)

Firminus. *Repertorium de mutatione aeris.* Paris, 1540.

Fleming, Abraham. *Of All Blasing Starrs in generall.* London, 1577, 1618. (See *Nausea.*)

Floridus, Ambrosius. *Tractatus de annis climactericis, ac diebus criticis.* Padua, 1612.

Fludd, Robert. *Utriusque Cosmi Maioris.* . . . Oppenhemii, 1617, 1619.

Fontaine, Jacques. *De astrologia medica liber.* Lyons, 1622.

Forte, A. *Dialogo delle comete.* . . . Venice, 1533.

Fracastoro, Girolamo. *De causis criticorum dierum.* Venice, 1538.

Frisius, Gemma. *De principiis astronomiae et cosmographiae.* Antwerp, 1530.

Frisius, Laurentius. *Expositio usuque astrolabii.* Strassburg, 1522.

Frytschius, Marcus. *De meteoris.* Nuremburg, 1563; Wittenburg, 1583.

——. *Catalogus prodigiorum miraculorum.* Nuremburg, 1563.

Fuscus, P. *De usu et abusu astrologiae in arte medica.* Rome, 1565.

Galen, Claudius. *De diebus decretoriis.* Lyons, 1533.

——. *Prognostica de decubitu infirmorum* (trans. Joseph Struthius). Lyons, 1550.

——. *Prognostica ex egroti decubitu* (trans. J. A. Mariscottus). Venice, 1584.

Gallucius, Giovanni Paolo. *De figura coelesti erigenda . . . De zodiaci divisione, De planetarum, . . . De temporibus ad medicandum accomodatis.* Venice, 1584.

——. *Theatrum mundi et temporis . . . ubi astrologiae principia cernuntur ad medicinam accomodata.* Venice, 1588, 1589, 1603; Grenada (Spanish eds.), 1600, 1612, 1617.

——. *Speculum uranicum.* . . . Venice, 1593.

Ganassonus, P. *Regule de electione et de astrologia.* . . . Briziae, 1505.

Ganivetus, Johannes. *Amicus medicorum.* Lyons, 1496, 1508, 1550, 1596; Frankfort, 1614.

Garcaeus, John. *Tractatus . . . de erigendis figures coeli, verificationibus, revolutionibus, et directionibus.* Wittenburg, 1556, 1573, 1575.

——. *De tempore.* Wittenburg, 1563.

——. *Meteorologia.* Wittenburg, 1568, 1584.

——. *Astrologiae methodus.* Basle, 1570, 1576, 1586.

Gauric, Luke. *Oratio de inventoribus & laudibus astrologiae.* Venice, 1531, 1540.

——. *Paraphrases & annotationes in Cl. Ptolomaei libro ii apotelesmaton.* Louvain?, 1539.

——. *Tractatus judicandi conversiones sive revolutiones nativitatum.* Venice, 1525?; Rome, 1560.

——. *Tractatus astrologiae judiciariae de nativitatibus virorum et mulierum.* Rome, 1539; Nuremburg, 1540; Venice, 1552, 1594.

——. *De diebus criticis . . . tractatus medicis. . . .* Rome, 1546.

——. *Schemata astrologica civitatum et illustrium virorum.* Venice, 1552.

——. *Opera astronomica et astrologica.* Basle, 1575.

Geber, John. *De astronomia per Gerardum Cremonensen.* Nuremburg, 1533; Ingolstadt, 1534.

Georgius Cracovius. *De utilitate astrologiae carmen. . . .* N.p., 1549.

Gilliszoon. (See *Aegidius.*)

Giuffus, Antonius. *De eclipsibus.* Naples, 1621.

Giuntini, Francesco. (See *Junctin.*)

Glogovia, Joannes de (John of Glogau). *Tractatus . . . in judiciis astrorum de mutationibus aeris.* Cracovie, 1514.

Goclenius, Rudolphus. *Aphorismorum chiromanticorum . . . addita est Praxis astrologica.* Lichae, 1597.

——. *Urania . . . astronomia et astrologia speciali. . . .* Frankfort, 1602; Marpurgi, 1614; Frankfort, 1615.

——. *Uranoscopiae, chiroscopiae, metoposcopiae, et ophthalmoscopiae, contemplatio.* Marpurgi, 1603; Frankfort, 1608; Prostat, 1618.

——. *Astrologia generalis.* Marpurgi, 1611, 1614.

——. *Acroteleution astrologicum.* Marpurgi, 1614, 1618.

——. *Synopsis geometriae, astronomiae, astrologiae, opticae, et geographiae.* Frankfort, 1620.

Godfridus (Erra Pater?). *The Boke of Knowledge of Thynges Unknowen Apperteynge to Astronomye.* London, 1530?, 1585, 1588, 1619.

Gordonius, Bernardus. *Lilium medicinae.* Frankfort, 1617.

Granollachs, Bernardo de. *De la nobilissima arte et scientia de astrologia.* Rome, 1485, 1488, 1500.

Grau, F. (See *Nausea.*)

Gregorius, P. *Syntaxes artis mirabilis. . . .* Lyons, 1575–1576.

Guarimbertus, Matthei. *De radiis planetarum.* Nuremburg, 1535.

Guasconus, Franciscus. *Judicum sive prognosticon astrologicum super principales mundi partes. . . .* Venice, 1474.

Guido, John. *De temporis astrorum . . . electionem item astrorum.* Paris, 1543.

Guillermin, A. *Briefve et succincte declaration que signifie le Soleil parmy les signes a la nativitie de l'enfant.* Lyons, 1546, 1556, 1580.

Gulielmus, H. A. *Institutiones philosophicae et astronomicae.* Basle, 1531.

Hagecius, Thaddaeus (Tadeus Hajek). *Astrologica opuscula antiqua fragmentum astrologicum.* Prague, 1564; Hague Comitum, 1564; Cologne, 1564.

Haghen, Theodoricus. *Prognosticum stellae.* Ultragecti, 1553.

Haly Rodan. *Commentarium in Quadripartitum Ptolomei, & centum aphorisms.* Venice, 1493.

Hartgill, George. *Astronomicall tables.* London, 1594.

Hartmann, T. *Lucenisis cometen spiegel.* Halle, 1605.

Harvey, John. *An Astrological Addition.* London, 1583.

Harvey, Richard. *An Astrological Discourse upon the great and notable Conjunction of the two superior Planets, Saturn and Jupiter.* London, 1583.

Haschardus, Petrus. *Clypeus astrologicus.* Louvain, 1552, 1554.

Henischius, G. *Prognosticum tempestatum ex ortu et occasu stellarum.* Augsburg, 1609.

Henrichman, J. *Prognostica. . . .* Strassburg, 1509.

Henricus Grammateus. *Tabulae cognoscendorum humanorum secundum motum planetarum.* Vienna, 1524.

Hephaisteion. (Ephestio) *Circulus solaris, de judiciis sive significationibus xii locorum orbis signiferi; De decretis planetarum, horumque natura; Medicationibus ad eas directis 1532.* Nuremburg, 1532.

Herlich, D. (David Hierlitius?) *Historiche Stern-Glocke von der grossen Convention Saturni und Jovis.* Stettin, 1603.

——. *Prognosticon astrologicum.* Stetini, 1619.

Hermes Trismegistus. *Centiloquium.* Venice, 1484, 1493; Leipsic, 1495; Venice, 1495, 1501, 1519; Basle, 1533, 1551; Prague, 1564.

——. *De decubitu infirmorum (Iatromathematica).* Nuremburg, 1532; Paris, 1555; Cologne, 1556, 1570; London, 1583 (trans. John Harvey); Venice, 1584; Augsburg, 1597.

——. *De revolutionibus nativitatum libro duo.* Augsburg, 1558; Basle, 1559.

——. *Pymander.* Trevisa, 1491; Florence, 1503, 1548; Lyons, 1570; Burdigalae, 1574; Cracoviae, 1584.

Hessus, H. *Astrologica.* Nuremburg, 1532.

Heurtevyn, B. *L'Incertitude et tromperie des astrologues judiciaires.* Paris, 1619.

Hill, Thomas. *A Contemplation of Mysteries: conteyning the rare effects and significations of Certayne Comets.* London, 1590?

Hippocrates. *Opusculum repertorii prognosticon in mutationes aeris tam via astrologica quam matheorologica.* Venice, 1485.

——. *Hippocrates libellus de medicorum astrologia.* Venice, 1485, 1497; Leipsic, 1505; Lyons, 1508; Venice, 1510; Cracovia, 1514; Verona, 1595.

——. *De significatione mortis, et vitae, secundum motum lunae, et aspectus planetarum.* Lyons, 1550.

Hooker, J. *The Events of Comets or Blazing Stars.* London, 1577.

Hossmann, A. *De natura et nativitate hominis.* Altenberg, 1613.

Hyginus. *Astronomicon.* Venice, 1484; Paris, 1559; Cologne, 1569.

Indagine, John. *Introductiones apotelesmaticae in chyromantium, physiognomiam, astrologiam naturalem.* Strassburg, 1522; Frankfort, 1522; Ursellis, 1522; Strassburg, 1531, 1534, 1541; Paris, 1543, 1545, 1547; Lyons, 1556, 1582; Ursellis, 1603; Strassburg, 1622.

——. *Briefe Introductions . . . in the Arte of Chiromancy, Physiognomy, Natural Astrology.* Trans. Fabian Withers. London, 1558, 1575, 1598, 1615.

Jackson, Hugh (printer). *The Husbandman's Practice; or, Prognostication for ever, as teacheth Alberte, Alkin, Haly, and Ptolemy.* London, n.d.

Jadertinus, Fredericus Chrisogonus. *Prognosticandi et currandi febres.* Venice, 1528.

Jergis (Gergius, Zergius). *De significatione planetarum in duodecim domibus.* Venice, 1509.

Joannes Hispalensis. (John of Spain) *Epitome totius astrologiae.* Nuremburg, 1548.

Johannes of Hassfurt. (See *Vindung.*)

Johannes of Verona. (See *Paduanius.*)

Junctin, Francis. (Francesco Giuntini) *Tractatus judicandi revolutiones nativitatum.* Lyons, 1570, 1581, 1583.

——. *Discorso in difesa dell' astrologia.* Lyons, 1571.

——. *Speculum astrologiae.* Lyons, 1573, 1581, 1583.

——. *Tractatio . . . de cometarum causis, effectibus, differentiis, et eorundem proprietatibus.* Lipsiae, 1580.

K., F. *Of the Crinitall Starre, . . .* London, 1580.

Kalender. *Compost et Kalendrier de bergiers.* Paris, 1493 (2 eds.), 1496, 1497; Geneva, 1497; Paris, 1499, 1500; Geneva, 1500; Lyons, 1502; Rouen, 1505; Lyons, 1508, 1510; Troyes, 1510; Lyons, 1513; Paris, 1523; Lyons, 1524; Troyes, 1529, 1541; Lyons, 1551; Paris, 1569, 1589.

——. *Kalender of Shepherdes* (English trans.). Paris, 1503; London, 1506, 1508, 1518, 1528, 1556, 1559, 1560, 1570, 1580, 1581, 1596, 1604, 1611, 1612.

Kepler, John. *Nova dissertatiumcula de fundamentis astrologiae.* Prague, 1602.

——. *De cometis, libelli tres: Astronomicus, Physicus, Astrologicus, de significationibus cometarum annorum 1607 et 1618.* Augsburg, 1619.

——. *Epitomes astronomie.* Frankfort, 1621.

——. *Discurs von der grossen Conjunction . . . Saturni und Jovis.* Lintz, 1623.

——. *De rebus astrologicis.* N.p., n.d.

Koebel, Jacob. *Astrolabii declaratio, . . . cui accessit isagogicon in astrologiam judiciarium.* Strassburg, 1545; Paris, 1550, 1551, 1552, 1585.

——. *Elucidarius von allerhand Geschopffen Gottes, den Engeln, den Himmeln, Gestirn, Planeten.* Frankfort, 1552, 1572, 1589.

Kollner, Johannes. *Tractatus physicus mathematicus.* Greifswald, 1618.

Lalamantius, Johannes. *De diebus decretoriis.* Lyons, 1560.

Lamchovius, J. *Opusculum de causis eclipsium et effectibus.* Gracchoviae, 1543.

Larivey, Pierre de. *Six centuries de predictions.* Lyons, 1623.

Laurentius, Andreas. *De crisibus.* Lyons, 1605.

Lemnius, Levinus. *De astrologiae.* Antwerp, 1554; Frankfort, 1596, 1608, 1626.

Leonardus, Camillus (Camillo Lunardi). *Speculum lapidum.* Venice, 1502, 1516; Augsburg, 1533; Paris, 1610. (Italian trans., 1565, 1617.)

Leovitius, Cyprianus. *Ephemerides, 1556–1606.* Augsburg, n.d.

——. *De eclipsibus, 1554–1606.* Augsburg, 1556.

——. *Brevis et Perspicua Ratio Judicandi Genitures ex Physicis causis et vera Experimenta Extracta.* London, 1558; Basle, 1559.

——. *De judiciis nativitatum doctrina.* (In *Astrologia aphoristica* of A. E. Strauchius, Lipsiae, 1712; cf. also *An Astrological Catechism . . . from Leovitius,* trans. Robert Turner, London, 1786.)

——. *De conjunctionibus magnis insignioribus superiorum planetarum, solis defectionibus et cometis, . . . cum eorundem effectum historica expositione.* Lauginae, 1564 (Latin and German eds.); Paris, 1568; London, 1573; Wittenburg, 1586; Marpurgi, 1618.

Leupoldus. *De astrorum scientia.* Augsburg, 1489; Venice, 1520.

Liber. *Liber novem judicum in judiciis astrorum. Clarissimi auctores istius voluminis: Meschella, Aomar, Alkindus, Zael, Albenait [Albohali], Dorotheus, Jergis, Aristotles, Ptholomaeus.* Venice, 1509.

Licetus, Fortunius. *De cometis.* Venice, 1623.

Lichtenberger, J. *Planeten Buchlein.* Frankfort, 1595.

Litchenberger, P. *Compendium duodecim domorum coelestium.* Basle, 1510.

Lindhout, Henricus. *Speculum astrologiae, in quo vera astrologiae fundamenta et genethliacal Arabum doctrinae vanitates demonstrantur.* Hamburg, 1597; Frankfort, 1608.

——. *Tractatus astrologicus, seu introductio in physicam judiciarum.* Hamburg, 1597, 1598; Lipsiae, 1618. (Dedicated to Queen Elizabeth of England.)

Longomontanus (Lumborg), C. Severinus. *Disputationes quatuor astrologicae.* Hafniae, 1622.

Lucian. *De astrologia.* Basle, 1527; Cracoviae, 1531; Antwerp, 1538; Paris, 1563.

Ludovicus de Regiis. *Aphorismi astrologici.* Nuremburg, 1535.

Lull, Raymond. *De astrologia, de medicina, de metaphysica, &c.* Lyons, 1523.

Lumborg. (See *Longomontanus.*)

Lungiano, F. de. *De gli auguri e de le superstitioni degl' antichi* . . . ; *quaranto otto osservationi regolate al moto della Luna.* Ulmae, 1542.

Maajus, T. *Historische warhafftige Beschreibung von den Cometen.* Magdeburg, 1619.

Maginus, Giovanni Antonio. *De astrologica ratione ac usu dierum criticorum seu decretoriorum.* Venice, 1607; Frankfort, 1608.

Maimonides, Moses. *Epistola de astrologia.* Cologne, 1555.

Manfredi, Girolamo di. *Centiloquium de medicis et infirmis.* Bononiae, 1489; Venice, 1500; Nuremburg, 1530.

——. *Liber de homine et conservatione sanitatis* (Italian eds., *Libro del Perche*). Bononiae, 1474; Naples, 1478; Bononiae, 1497; Venice, 1512, 1514, 1520, 1523, 1530, 1588, 1591, 1607, 1622.

Manginus, C. A. *Astrorum simulacra.* Bononiae, 1625.

Manilius, Marcus. *Astronomicon.* Venice, 1474, 1484, 1489, 1490, 1499, 1503; Basle, 1533, 1551; Lyons, 1566, 1579, 1584; Antwerp, 1590; Plantiniana, 1600; Lyons, 1600; Antwerp, 1600.

Manzoni, F. *Discorso astrologico.* Verona, 1617.

Maplet, John. *The Diall of Destiny.* London, 1581, 1582.

Marius, G. A. *Astronomicum judicium.* Nuremburg, 1615.

Marstaller, Gervasius. *Artis divinatricis, quam astrologiam seu judiciarium vocant.* Paris, 1549.

Maternus, Julius Firmicus. *De nativitatibus, sive Matheseos libri viii.* Venice, 1497, 1499, 1503; Basle, 1533, 1551. (Called also *Astronomicon libri viii.*) (Partial ed., Bks. iii–v, Venice, 1488, 1494.)

Melanchthon, Philip. *Orationes aliquot lectu dignissimae.* Haganoae, 1533.

——. *Initia doctrina physicae dictata in academia Witebergense.* Wittenburg, 1549, 1550; Basle, 1549; Frankfort, 1550; Lyons, 1552; Wittenburg, 1585.

——. *Claudii Ptolamaei, De praedictionibus astronomicis, cui titulum fecerunt Quadripartitum.* Basle, 1553.

——. *Procli paraphrasis in quatuor Ptolamaei libros de siderum effectionibus.* Basle, 1554.

Messahala. *De receptionibus planetarum; De interrogationibus; Epistola de junctionibus planetarum; De revolutionibus anno mundi.* Basle?, 1493.

——. *De scientia motus orbis.* Nuremburg, 1504.

——. *Ptholomeus de electionibus.* Venice, 1509; Paris, 1513.

——. *Libri tres, . . . De revolutione annorum, De significatione planetarum in nativitatibus, De receptione. . . .* Nuremburg, 1549.

——. *De elementis et orbitus coelestibus liber.* Nuremburg, 1549.

——. (See *Liber.*)

Michael of Breslau. *Introductorium astronomie.* Cracoviae, 1513, 1517.

Milich, Jacob. *Oratio de dignitate astrologiae . . . in promotione magistorum.* Hagenau, 1533, 1538, 1546; Paris, 1549.

——. *Propositiones medicae.* N.p., 1552.

Mizauld, Antony. *Harmonia superioris nature mundi et inferioris. . . .* Paris, 1555, 1577.

——. *Harmonia coelestium corporum et humanorum dialogis undecim astronomice et medice. . . .* Paris, 1555, 1556; Lyons, 1580; Frankfort, 1589; Paris, 1592; Frankfort, 1599.

——. *Aesculapii et uraniae medicum simul et astronomocum ex colloquio conjugium harmoniam microcosmi cum macrocosmo.* Lyons, 1550.

——. *Ephemerides perpetuelles de l'air, autrement l'astrologie rustiques. . . .* Paris, 1546, 1547, 1554; Antwerp, 1547, 1556, 1560; Lutetiae, 1554.

——. *Asterismi: sive, Stellatarum octavi coeli imaginum officina.* Paris, 1553.

——. *Zodiacus: sive, Duodecim signorum coeli hortulus.* Paris, 1553.

——. *Planetae: sive, Planetarum collegium.* Paris, 1553.

——. *Cometographia.* Paris, 1549.

——. *Planetographia rebus astronomicus, medicis et philosophicis erudite referta.* Lyons, 1551.

——. *L'Explication, usage et practica de l'Ephemeride celeste.* Paris, 1556.

——. *Meteorologia, sive rerum aeriarum commentariolus.* Paris, 1547, 1548.

——. *Les lovanges antiquitez et excellences d'astrologie.* Paris, 1563.

——. *Secrets de la Luna opuscule.* Paris, 1571.

——. *Paradoxa rerum coeli.* Paris, 1576, 1577.

——. *De legitimo astrologiae in medicina usu.* Venice, 1607.

Moller, T. *Astrologia judiciaria.* Frankfort, 1581.

Mollerius, Elias. *De eclipsibus.* N.p., 1607.

Monantheuil, Henri de. *Ludus iatromathematicus.* Paris, 1597.

Monte Ulmi, Antonius de. *Libellus de astrologia judiciaria.* Nuremburg, 1540.

——. *A ryghte excellent treatise of astronomie.* Trans. Frederike van Brunswicke. London, 1554.

Morinus, J. B. *Astronomicarum domorum cabala detecta.* Paris, 1623.

Morshemius, Johannes Mercurius. *De judiciis astrologicis.* Basle, 1558, 1559.

Moulton, Thomas. *The Myrrour or glasse of helthe.* London, 1539 (2 eds.), 1540 (4 eds.), 1541 (2 eds.), 1545, 1546, 1550 (2 eds.), 1565, 1580.

Muller, John. (See *Regiomontanus.*)

Muller, Phillip. *De cometa.* Lipsiae, 1619.

Mullerius, Nicolaus. *Institutionum astronomicarum libri duo.* Groningae, 1616.

Mulmann, J. *De natura coeli et praecipuis eius affectionibus.* Lipsiae, 1608.

Munoz, G. *Institutiones arithmeticae ad percipiendam astrologiam et mathematicas facultates necessariae.* Valenciae, 1566.

Munz, J. *Prognostica a stellis sumpta.* Vindobonae, 1500?

Murer, Wolfgang. *Meteorologica.* Lipsiae, 1588.

Nabod, Valentine. *Ennaratio elementorum astrologiae.* Cologne, 1560, 1566.

——. *De coelo & terra, lib. 3.* Venice, 1573.

——. *In Cl. Ptolomaei Quadripartitae . . . commentarius.* Venice, 1607. (At end of Magini's *De astrologica ratione;* is commentary on only Bk. III, chs. 10–11.)

Nagel, P. *Completum astrologiae.* Halle, 1620.

Nausea, Fredericus (F. Grau). *Of All Blasing Starrs in generall.* Trans. Abraham *Fleming.* London, 1577, 1618.

Neri, G. de. *Trattato . . . pronostici universali.* Verona, 1600.

Niphus, Augustinus. *Medici ac astrologi . . . de diebus criticis.* Venice, 1504, 1518, 1519; Strassburg, 1528; Marpurgi, 1614, 1616.

——. *Ad apotelesmata Ptolemaei eruditiones.* Naples, 1513.

——. *De prognostics, liber tertius.* Marpurgi, 1614.

——. *De medicamentorum electionibus.* Marpurgi, 1614.

Obicius, Hippolitus. *Tractatus medici et astronomici, . . . opuscula de astrologia.* Venice, 1618.

——. *Iatrastronomicon.* Venice, 1618.

——. *Dialogus Tripartius.* Venice, 1605; Mainz, 1619.

Offusius, Joannes Francus. *De divina astrorum facultate in larvatam astrologiam.* Paris, 1570, 1579.

Omar ben Alphorkhan. *Liber de nativitatibus et interrogationibus.* Venice, 1503, 1509, 1515, 1524, 1525; Basle, 1551.

Origanus, D. (Trost or Dost) *Brevis ac utilis themathographia, continens compositionem et usum tabularum domorum.* Frankfort, 1614.

Paceus, J. *Astrologia vindicata.* N.p., 1562.

Paduanius, Johannes. (of Verona) *Opusculum de usu horoscopii.* Venice, 1560, 1563; Verona, 1560, 1592.

——. *Viridarium mathematicorum.* Venice, 1563.

——. *De singularum humani corporis partium significatibus.* Verona, 1589.

Paracelsus. *Astronomica et astrologia.* Cologne, 1567.

——. *Astronomia magna . . . die Mysterien der himmlischen Licht was die Geister durch der Menschen wirken.* Frankfort, 1571.

Partlicius, Simon. *Mundus furiosus.* Rostick, 1622.

——. *De influentis.* Rostock?, 1623.

Pater, Erra. *Book of Knowledge, Treating of the Wisdom of the Ancients.* London, 1530?, 1585, 1588, 1619. (See *Godfridus.*)

Paulus, Alexandrinus. *Rudimenta in doctrinam de praedictis natalitius.* Wittenburg, 1586, 1588.

Peletier, Jacques. *Medici et mathematici . . . de constitutione horoscopi.* Basle, 1563.

Persona, J. B. *Noctes solitariae liber, . . . in duo . . . theologica, physica, metaphysica, ethica, medica, geometrica, astronomica, demum, et physiognomonica.* Venice, 1613.

Peucer, Caspar. *De astrologia.* Wittenburg, 1553, 1560, 1571, 1572, 1576, 1580; Lyons, 1584; Antwerp, 1584; Frankfort, 1593, 1607.

Pezel, Christopher. *Praecepta genethliaca, sive de prognosticandis hominum nativitatibus.* Frankfort, 1607.

Philomusus (B. Carrichter von Reckingen). *Krauterbuch.* . . . Strassburg, 1573, 1575, 1576, 1619.

Pianero, Giolanni. *Dubitationum et solutionum in III Galeni de diebus criticis liber unus; In eundem tertium Galeni de diebus criticis scholia.* Venice, 1574.

Pisani, Ottavio. *Astrologia seu motus et loco siderum ad seren dominum cosmum medicen.* Antwerp, 1613.

Pitatus, Petrus. *Almanach novum. Isagogica in coelestem astronomicam disciplinam. Tractatus . . . electionibus revolutionibus annorum et mutatione aeris.* Tubingen, 1544, 1548, 1552, 1553.

Planer, J. A. *Das grosse Planeten-Buch, welches aus dem Platone, Ptolomeo, Hali, Albumasar, Konigsperger, . . . nebst Geomantie, Physiognomie under Chiromantie, wie, auch alter Weiber Philosophie.* Frankfort, 1580; Strassburg, 1597?; Amsterdam, 1600; Strassburg, 1619.

Pontanus, J. Joviani. *De rebus coelestibus.* Venice, 1519; Basle, 1530, 1538.

——. *In Centum Ptolomei Aphorismos commentatio.* Basle, 1531.

——. *Quatenus credendum sit astrologis.* Cologne, 1544.

——. *Urania.* Basle, 1556.

——. *Astrologia proverbialis.* Frankfort, 1583.

——. *Opera omnia.* Venice, 1518–1519; Basle, 1566.

Porta, Giovanni Battista della. *Coelestis physiognomiae libri vi.* Naples, 1601, 1603; Strassburg, 1606; Padova, 1616, 1623.

——. *De humana physiognomia.* Naples?, 1586, 1588, 1593.

Porphirius. *In Ptolomeum.* Basle, 1559.

Postel, Guillaume. *Signorum coelestium vera configuratio aut asterimus.* Paris, 1553.

Proclus. *Paraphrasis in quatuor Ptolemaei in libros de siderum effectionibus.* Basle, 1535, 1554, 1559.

Ptholomaeus. *The Compost of Ptholomaeus Prynce of Astronomye.* London, 1532?, 1535?, 1538, 1540?

——. (See *Liber.*)

Ptolemy, Claudius. *Quadripartitum.* Venice, 1484, 1493, 1519; Paris, 1519; Basle, 1533; Nuremburg, 1535 (Bk. I); Louvain, 1539; Basle, 1540, 1541; Louvain, 1548; Lyons, 1549 (Bk. I); Basle, 1551, 1553, 1554; Lyons, 1554; Basle, 1555, 1559, 1568, 1573, 1578, 1579; Lyons, 1581, 1583; Basle, 1583; Prague, 1610.

——. *Centiloquium.* Venice, 1484, 1493, 1519; Basle, 1533, 1535; Rome, 1540; Cologne, 1544; Basle, 1550, 1551, 1553; Venice, 1565; Lyons, 1581; Basle, 1583.

——. *Inerrantium stellarum significationibus.* Venice, 1515; Basle, 1533; Wittenburg, 1534, 1547; Lyons, 1547; Basle, 1551, 1568; Urbini, 1592.

Rantzovius, Henricus. *Catalogus imperatorum regum ac principum qui astrologicam artem amarunt.* Antwerp, 1580; Lipsiae, 1584; Cologne, 1585.

——. *Catalogue imperatorum regum ac virorum illustrium qui artem astrologicam amarunt.* Lipsiae, 1584.

——. *Tractatus astrologicus de genethliacorum thematum judiciis pro singulis nati accidentibus. Secunda editio.* Oldenburg, 1591; Wittenburg, 1594; Frankfort, 1595, 1600, 1602, 1615, 1625.

——. *Exempla quibus astrologicae scientiae. . . . Item de annis climactericis et periodis imperiorum, cum pluribus aliis artem astrologicam illustrantibus.* Cologne, 1585. (3rd. ed.)

——. *Horoscopographia.* Strassburg, 1585; Wittenburg, 1586, 1588.

——. *Calendarium . . . in usum mediocorum quam astrologorum.* Hamburg, 1590.

——. *Thematum coelestium . . . astrologiae judiciariae.* Frankfort, 1611.

Raspe, G. *Dissertatio de stellarum natura earunque affectionibus in genere.* Lipsiae, 1620.

——. *De natura coeli et praecipus eius affectionibus.* Lipsiae, 1621.

Rastell, J. *Canones astrologici.* London, 1525?

Rauchfuss. (See *Dasypodius.*)

Reckingen. (See *Philomusus.*)

Reges. *Liber de significationibus planetarum in xii domiciliis coeli, et de natura xii signorum zodiaci.* Prague, 1564; Hague Comitum, 1564; Cologne, 1564.

Regiomontanus. (John Muller) *Tabulae directionum . . . astrologiae judiciariae.* Augsburg, 1490; Nuremburg, 1552; Wittenburg, 1606.

Reisch, Gregorius. *Margarita philosophia . . . contineantur . . . Astrologiae, Necromantia, Geomantia, artem Notoria, Alchemae, &c.* Strassburg, 1503, 1504; Basle, 1533; Venice, 1599. (And many other editions.)

Rhasis, A. *Liber ad Almansorem libri x.* Venice, 1497, 1510.

Ringelbergius, J. F. *Astrologicarum institutionum libri iii.* Paris, 1530.

——. *Astrologia cum geomantia et physiognomia.* Lyons, 1531.

——. *Opera.* Basle, 1538, 1541; Lyons, 1556.

Rizza Casa, G. *Trattato di naturale astrologia giudiciaria.* Lyons, 1591.

Rocha, Thomas. *Compilatio quedam terminorum astronomie. Compilatio quaedam in eligendo tempus corpori humano in exibitione medicinarum.* Montpellier, 1501.

Roffendi, G. Antonio. *Discorso astrologico.* Bologna, 1618.

Roglitz, M. B. von. *Bewegungen der Planeten, und ihre Wirkungen auf menschlichen Leben.* Leipsig, 1594.

Rossi, Gioseppe de. *Discorso sopra gli anni climaterici.* Rome, 1585.

Rossaccio, G. *Il medico . . . astrologia.* Venice, 1621.

Roslin, Helisaeus. *Hypotheses de mundo.* Frankfort, 1587.

Rothmann, John. *Concordantia genethliaca cum chyromantia.* Erfurt, 1595, 1596.

Roussat, Richard. *Des elemens et principes d'astronomie, avec les universels jugemens d'icelle.* Paris, 1552.

Ruberti, B. de. *Osservazione de astrologia . . . medicina.* Florence, 1567.

Ryff, Walther Hermann. *Iatromathematicae . . . enchirdion. . . .* Strassburg, 1542.

Sadeler, Jan. *Planetarum effectus et eorum in signis zodiaci super provincias, regiones, et civitates dominia.* Antwerp, 1585.

Salius, G. *De nobilitate astrologiae.* Venice, 1519.

Sanctus, C. *Opusculum de magnorum luminarium conjunctionibus, oppositionibus, et quadraturis.* Rome, 1571.

Santritter, J. L. *De judiciis nativitatum.* Venice, 1494.

Sarcocephalus, G. *Duodecim domiciliorum coelestium tabula nova.* Vratislaviae, 1600.

Sarzosus, F. *Commentarius in aequatorem planetarum.* Paris, 1526, 1535, 1581, 1590.

Satler, Wolfgang. *Dianoia astrologica . . . accessit . . . succincta exegesis astrologica.* Montisbeligardi, 1605.

Saulnier, J. *Cosmologie du monde. . . .* Paris, 1618.

Scepperius, Cornelius. *De significationibus conjunctionum superiorum planetarum, &c. libri vi.* Antwerp, 1523; Cologne, 1548.

Schmidt, Johann Isaac. *Decas questionum illustrium astronomicarum et astrologicarum.* Wittenburg, 1625.

Schoner, John. *In vigenti octo mansiones Lunae . . . collectanea.* Nuremburg, 1530.

——. *Horoscopium generale omni regioni accomodatum.* Nuremburg, 1535.

——. *Opusculum astrologicum.* Nuremburg, 1539.

——. *Tractatus astrologicum judiciariae de nativitatibus.* Nuremburg, 1540.

——. *De judiciis nativitatum libri tres.* Nuremburg, 1545. (Italian trans., Venice, 1554.)

——. *Opera mathematica.* Nuremburg, 1551.

Scholl, Jacob. *Astrologiae ad medicinam adplicatio brevis.* Strassburg, 1537.

Schonheintz, Jacob. *Apologia astrologiae.* Nuremburg, 1502.

Schylander, Cornelius. *Medicina astrologica.* Antwerp, 1570, 1577.

Scot, Michael. *Mensa philosophica.* Lipsiae, 1603.

Servet, N. (See *Villanovanus.*)

Severinius, F. P. F. *Theses de natura corporis coelestis eiusque affectionibus et proprietatibus.* Heidelberg, 1610.

Shakelton, Francis. *A blazyng Starre or burnyng Beacon. . . .* London, 1580.

Shepherdes. (See *Kalender.*)

Siderocrates, Samuel (Eisenmenger). *De methodo medicorum et mathe-maticorum.* Tubingae, 1561, 1563.

——. *De usu partium coeli in commendationem astronomiae.* Tubingae, 1563; Strassburg, 1567.

Simus, N. *Tractatus de electionibus, de mutatione aeris, de revolutionibus annorum, et alia.* Venice, 1554.

Smoll, Godfridus. *Philosophica & medica pryncipia.* Lubecae, 1609.

Stabius, Johannes. *Horoscopion.* Nuremburg, 1512.

Stadius, Johannes. *Ephemerides, 1554-1570.* Cologne, 1556, 1570. (Contains the *Iatromathematica* of Hermes Trismegistus.)

Stanhuffius, Michael. *De meteoris.* Wittenburg, 1562.

Taisnier, John. *Astrologiae judiciariae isagoge.* Cologne, 1559.

——. *Opus mathematicum . . . cheiromantiae, physiognomiae, et natu-ralem astrologiam, . . . astrologiae judiciariae.* Cologne, 1562, 1583.

Tanner, Adam. *Orationes . . . de astrologia sacra.* Ingolstadt, 1615.

——. *Dissertatio de coelis.* Ingolstadt, 1621.

Tanner, Robert. *On the Conjunction of Saturne and Jupiter, 1583.* London, 1583.

——. *A Mirror for Mathematiques; . . . also a playne and most easie in-struction for the erection of a Figure for the 12 Houses of the Heavens.* London, 1587.

Tannstetter, George Collimitus. *Artificium de applicatione astrologie ad medicina.* Strassburg, 1531.

Taxil, J. *L'Astrologie et physiognomie en leur splendeur.* Tournon, 1614.

Theophrastus. *De signis temporum.* Venice, 1477, 1498; Basle, 1541; Paris, 1557; Lyons, 1613.

——. *De ventis.* Urbini, 1593.

Thomas, B. *De judiciis astrorum.* Liptzk, 1511.

Thurinus, Andreas. *Hippocrates et Galen defensio adversus Hieronymum Fracastorium, de causis dierum criticorum.* Rome, 1542.

Thurneiffe, Leonardus. *Virtutes planetarum influentiales.* Berlin, 1578.

——. *Kalendarium & Ephemeris.* Berlin, 1582.

Torella, Gaspar. *Judicium universale de portentis, praesagiis, ostentis et rerum admirabilium, ac solis et lunae defectibus atque cometis.* Rome, 1507; Tegernseensi, 1578; Frankfort, 1597.

Torporleius, Nathaniel. *Valvae astronomicae universales.* London, 1602.

Torella, Jerome Hieronymous. *Opus praeclarum de imaginibus astrologicis.* Valencia, 1496.

Torres, A. G. de. *Breve compendio de las alabancoes de la astrologia.* Toleto, 1524.

Trapezuntius, Georgius. *In Centum Ptolomei Aphorismos.* Venice, 1524; Cologne, 1544.

Trithemius, J. *Wunderbuch von der gottlichen Magie, dem Planeten und*

*Geburtsstunden-Einfluss der Signatur der Krauter, Mineralien, Thiere und Menschen, dem Universal-Spiritus.* Passau, 1506.

Tucciis, J. F. de. *Liber I de parte horoscopante ad Francis cum medicem, cum ipsius natali.* Lyons, 1585.

Turrel, Pierre. *Tractatus de cognoscendis infirmitatibus.* Lyons, 1525.

——. *Computus novus.* . . . Paris, 1525, 1526.

——. *Le Periode, c'est-a-dire la fin du monde contenant la disposition des chouses terrestres par la vertu et influence des corps celestes.* Lyons, 1531.

Twyne, Thomas. *A View of certain wonderful effects . . . of the Comete, or blasing Star, which appeared . . . 1577.* London, 1578.

Tyard, Pontus. *Mantice or discours de la verite de devination par astrologie.* Lyons, 1558; Paris, 1573.

Uttenhofer, K. *Judicium de nupero cometa astrologo-historicum, Kurtzer Bericht.* Nuremburg, 1619.

Valens, V. *Ex primo libro Floridorum de natura planetarum.* Nuremburg, 1532.

Valentinus, B. P. *De magia, de observatione somniorum et de divinatione astrologica.* Cologne, 1598.

Valla, Georgius. *De expetendis et fugiendis rebus opus, . . . de arithmetica, musica, geometria, astrologia, &c.* Venice, 1501.

——. *Commentationes in Ptolomei Quadripartitum.* Venice, 1502.

Vegius, M. *Geburstunden Buch.* Basle, 1570.

Venceslaus Cracoviensis. *Introductorium astrologiae compendiosum.* Cracoviae, 1515.

Verner, Noricus J. *Canones de mutatione aurae.* Nuremburg, 1546.

Vespucius, Bartolomeus. *Oratio de laudibus astrologiae.* Venice, 1508, 1513, 1518, 1531.

Villanovanus, M. (Michael Servet) *In quendam medicum apologetica disceptatio pro astrologia.* Paris, 1538.

Virdung, Johann (of Hassfurt). *Medici ac astrologi praestant, de cognoscendis et medendis morbis ex corporum coelestium positione, libri IIII.* Venice, 1584.

——. *Nova medicinae methodus nunc primum et condita et aedita ex mathematica ratione curandi.* N.P., 1532.

Wagner, Tobias. *Astrologia genethliaca.* Stuttgart, 1616.

Winckler, Nicolas. *Tractatus de astrologiae.* Frankfort, 1580.

Wolf, Hieronymous. *Admonitio de vero astrologiae usu.* London, 1558.

——. *Commentarii Ptolomaici et Porphyriana isagoge, cum Hermete de revolutionibus.* Basle, 1559.

Zael. (See *Liber.*)

Zeysius, M. *Prognosticon physicum astrologicum.* N.p., 1576.

Zimara, Marco Antonio. *Antrum magico-medicum.* . . . *constellationes astrorum cum signatura planetarum constitutarum.* Frankfort, 1575–1576, 1625.

Zinckius, Johannes. *De crisibus.* Frankfort, 1609.

Zobali, Alphonsus. *Speculum astrologice.* Bologna, 1623.

——. *De directionibus.* Vicentiae, 1620; Padova, 1621.

Zynthius, A. *De astrologorum observatione siderum.* Upsaliae, 1624.

Anonymous (?). *Arati Phaenomena et prognostica.* Basle, 1534, 1547; Paris, 1559; Cologne, 1569. (Alexandrinus Periegetes Dionysius?)

——. *Judicum cum tractatibus planetariis compositum.* . . . *Mediolani,* 1496. (Franciscus Guasconus?)

——. *Das gross Planetenbuch.* . . . Frankfort, 1558. (J. A. Planer?)

——. *Prognostication des hommes et des femmes de leurs nativities et influence selon les xii signes de l'an &c.* N.p., 1530?

——. *Methodii revelationes.* Basle, 1498.

——. *Die Kunst der Chiromantzen, Naturlichen Astrologey,* . . . Strassburg, 1523. (John Indagine?)

——. *Livre merveilleux.* . . . Paris, 1565, 1569, 1588.

——. *Les predictions remarquables de l'astrologue francois.* Paris, 1625.

——. *Astrologie naturelle.* . . . Paris, 1619.

——. *Astronomischen und mathematischen instrumenten.* Frankfort, 1564, 1619.

——. *Astronomisches und astrologisches Handbuch.* . . . Laugingen, 1609.

——. *Centiloquium de medicis et infirmis decerptum ex penetralibus astrologiae. Naturalis astrologiae compendiosa descriptio.* Cracoviae, 1532.

——. *Le traicte des comettes et significations d'icelles, extraict des ditz de Ptholomee, Albumazar, Haly, Alquindus, et autres astrologues.* Paris, 1540.

——. *Des comettes et leurs significances,* . . . *selon Ptolemee, Albumasar, Haly, et autres astrologues.* N.p., 1556.

——. *Della significatione de planeti quando sono signiori delle hore, &c.* Venice, 1578; Tubingae, 1559 (or 1579).

# INDEX